LIB051005 R3/78

FRASER UNIVERSITY LIBRARY

DATE DUE

S.F.U. MAR 7 1975

REC'D APR

REC'D APR

REC'D DEC 1 0 1980

D0941008

SOUTHEAST ASIA

William A. Withington

Dr. William A. Withington is known internationally as a geographer and as an author of geographical articles on Southeast Asia. He is Associate Professor of Geography at the University of Kentucky. Dr. Withington has spent two and one-half years in research and teaching in Sumatra, and has traveled extensively in Southeast Asia. He is a member of the Association of American Geographers and the Association of Asian Studies.

Margaret Fisher

Margaret Fisher is an author and editor of textbooks. She has also traveled extensively in Asia. As a former teacher, she is keenly aware of the needs and interests of elementary and secondary school students.

THE FIDELER COMPANY Grand Rapids, Michigan / Toronto, Canada

SOUTHEAST ASIA

CONTRIBUTORS

L. A. PETER GOSLING
Professor of Geography
Director, Center for Southeast
Asian Studies
University of Michigan
Ann Arbor, Michigan

WALDO R. TOBLER
Professor of Geography
University of Michigan
Ann Arbor, Michigan

ROBERT H. BAUER
Art Director

DONNA MOUL
Map Supervisor

JOEL BEVERSLUIS
Manuscript Editor

CONNIE J. NEGARAN
Manuscript Editor

DEBORAH BOLT
Picture Editor

CAROL S. PRESCOTT
Staff Writer

RAYMOND E. FIDELER
Editor and President

BEV J. ROCHE
Design Editor

MARY MITUS
Map Editor

MARION H. SMITH
Staff Writer

PETER J. VACCARO
Project Editor

COPYRIGHT, 1972

THE FIDELER COMPANY

All rights reserved in the U.S.A. and foreign countries. This book or parts thereof must not be reproduced in any form without permission. Printed in the U.S.A. by offset lithography.

Earlier Edition Copyright The Fideler Company 1968.

LIBRARY OF CONGRESS CATALOG CARD NUMBER: 72-76884

Bangkok, the capital of Thailand, is located along a river called the Chao Phraya. Among the hundreds of beautiful religious buildings in Bangkok is Wat Arun, whose golden tower you can see in this picture.

CONTENTS

Rice fields on the island of Java, in Indonesia.

A Global View of Asia

If you could view the earth from a space station, you would notice that its curved surface is covered mainly with water. Lying like enormous islands in the water are several great masses of land. By far the largest of these masses is Eurasia, which is located on the opposite side of the earth from North America.

Man has been living in Eurasia for at least one million years. Long ago, the people in the westernmost part of this landmass developed a civilization that differed greatly from the civilizations in the eastern part. As time went on, the western part of Eurasia came to be called Europe. The rest of this landmass came to be known as Asia, or the East. Geographers today generally agree that Europe and Asia are divided by an imaginary line that extends from the Caspian Sea northward along the Ural Mountains to the Arctic Ocean. To the south, Europe and Asia are separated by the Caucasus Mountains and by the Black and Aegean seas. (See map at right.)

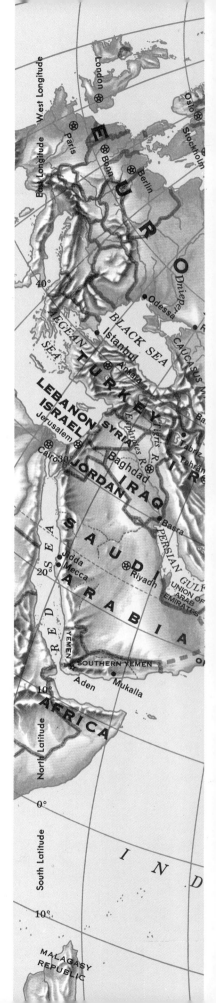

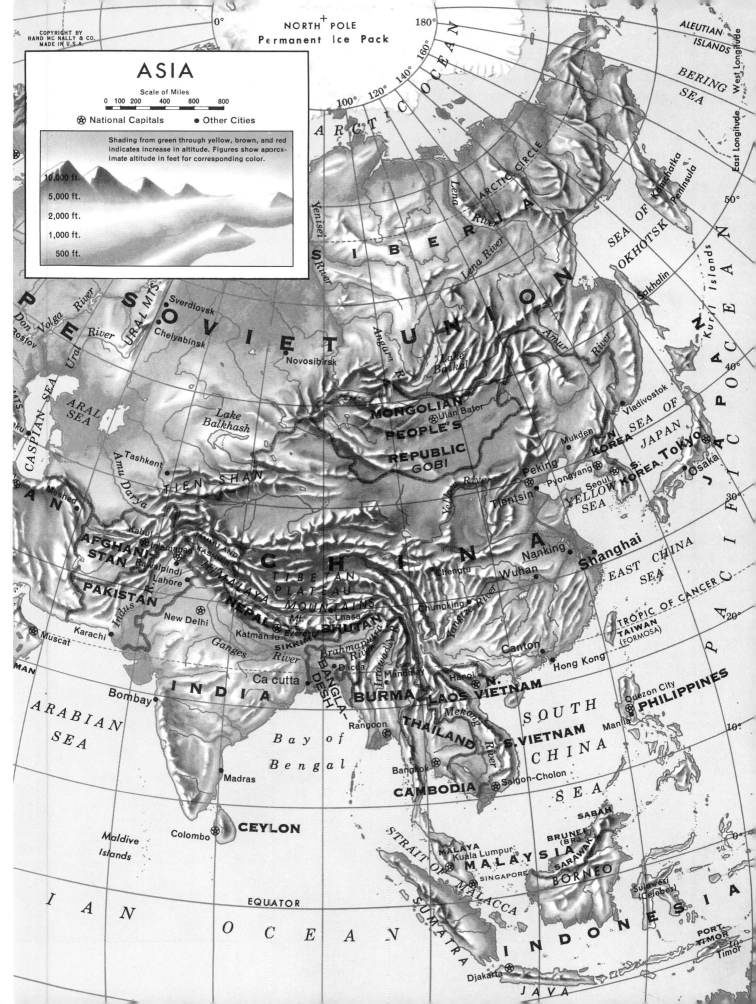

ASIA

Scale of Miles

0 100 200   400   600   800

⊛ National Capitals   • Other Cities

Shading from green through yellow, brown, and red
indicates increase in altitude. Figures show aporox-
imate altitude in feet for corresponding color.

10,000 ft.

5,000 ft.

2,000 ft.

1,000 ft.

500 ft.

COPYRIGHT BY
RAND MC NALLY & CO.
MADE IN U.S.A.

NORTH POLE
Permanent Ice Pack

ARCTIC OCEAN

ALEUTIAN
ISLANDS

BERING
SEA

ARCTIC CIRCLE

SIBERIA

Yenisei R. River

Lena River

Angara R.

Lena River

Amur River

SEA OF
OKHOTSK

Kamchatka
Peninsula

Kuril Islands

Sakhalin

PERSIA

URAL MTS.

Sverdlovsk

Chelyabinsk

Novosibirsk

SOVIET   UNION

Lake
Baikal

MONGOLIAN
PEOPLE'S
REPUBLIC

Ulan Bator

GOBI

Amur River

Vladivostok

SEA OF
KOREA
N.
KOREA

JAPAN

Tokyo

Osaka

PACIFIC   OCEAN

Don River
Rostov

Volga River

Ural River

Ural River

CASPIAN SEA

ARAL
SEA

Lake
Balkhash

Amu Darya

Tashkent

TIEN   SHAN

Mukden

Peking

Tientsin

Pyongyang

Seoul
S. KOREA

YELLOW
SEA

Baku

Meshed

AN

Kabul

AFGHANI-
STAN

Islamabad

Rawalpindi

Lahore

JAMMU AND
KASHMIR

HIMALAYA

CHINA

TIBETAN
PLATEAU

Yellow River

Chengtu

Wuhan

Nanking

Shanghai

EAST CHINA
SEA

TROPIC OF CANCER

PAKISTAN

Indus

Karachi

New Delhi

NEPAL

MOUNTAINS

Mt.
Everest

Lhasa

BHUTAN

Brahmaputra R.

Katmandu

SIKKIM

Chungking

Yangtze River

Canton

Hong Kong

TAIWAN
(FORMOSA)

Muscat

Ganges
River

BANGLA-
DESH

Dacca

Irrawaddy

Hanoi

N.
VIETNAM

Mandalay

SOUTH

PHILIPPINES

Quezon City

Bombay

INDIA

Calcutta

BURMA

LAOS

VIETNAM

Manila

OMAN

ARABIAN
SEA

Bay of
Bengal

Madras

Rangoon

THAILAND

Mekong River

S. VIETNAM

CHINA

SEA

Bangkok

Saigon-Cholon

SABAH

CAMBODIA

Colombo

CEYLON

Maldive
Islands

STRAIT OF MALACCA

MALAYA

Kuala Lumpur

MALAYSIA

BRUNEI
(BR.)

SARAWAK

BORNEO

Sulawesi
(Celebes)

SINGAPORE

INDIAN

EQUATOR

OCEAN

SUMATRA

INDONESIA

PORT.
TIMOR

Timor

Djakarta

JAVA

The world's largest continent. Asia is larger than any of the other continents on the earth. It extends from below the equator to above the Arctic Circle, and stretches nearly halfway around the world. About one third of the total land surface of the globe is included in this giant continent. The map on pages vi and vii shows that there are many different countries in Asia. Some are large and some are very small.

A continent of contrasts. The vast continent of Asia is a land of contrasts. As the map on pages vi and vii shows, a cluster of towering mountains and high plateaus rises in the south central part of this continent. From this highland cluster, other mountain ranges and plateaus stretch out in several directions. These highland barriers help to divide Asia into six main regions. (See opposite page.)

A shepherd in the Himalaya Mountains. The Himalayas are part of a cluster of towering mountains and high plateaus in south central Asia. Find these and other highlands of Asia on the map on pages vi and vii. In what parts of this continent are the largest lowland areas located?

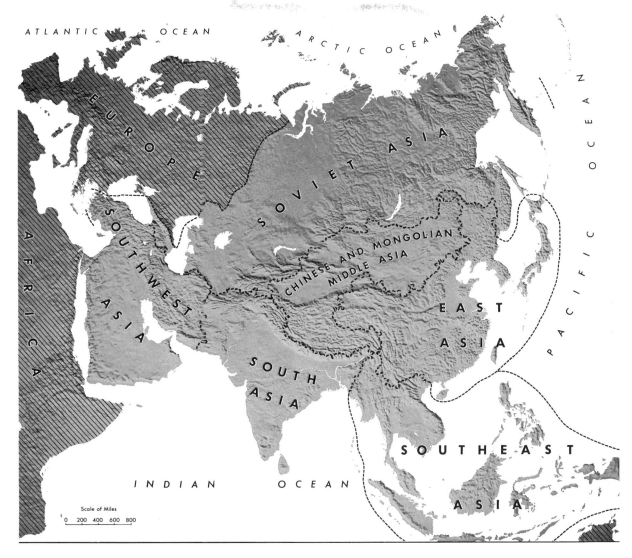

REGIONS OF ASIA

South Asia includes the large, triangular-shaped peninsula on which the countries of India, Pakistan, and Bangladesh are located, the island country of Ceylon, and the four mountainous countries of Afghanistan, Nepal, Sikkim, and Bhutan. It is one of the most densely populated parts of the world.

Chinese and Mongolian Middle Asia includes the Mongolian People's Republic as well as Sinkiang, Inner Mongolia, and Tibet, which are controlled by China. It is a thinly populated region of deserts, grasslands, plateaus, and high mountains.

Soviet Asia includes Siberia, Soviet Middle Asia, and Transcaucasia. Siberia has been settled mainly by immigrants from the European part of the Soviet Union. The people in the other two areas have much in common with people in neighboring parts of Asia.

Southeast Asia is a tropical, rainy region of islands and peninsulas. It includes the countries of Burma, Thailand, Cambodia, Laos, North and South Vietnam, Malaysia, Singapore, Indonesia, and the Philippines.

Southwest Asia includes Turkey, Iran, Iraq, Syria, Lebanon, Israel, Jordan, the countries and territories on the Arabian peninsula, and the island of Cyprus. Archaeologists believe civilization may have begun in this dry, rugged region. Three of the world's great religions—Judaism, Christianity, and Islam—began here. The world's largest reserves of oil are located in this region.

East Asia includes Japan, North and South Korea, and part of China. Taiwan and Hong Kong are located here also. More people live in East Asia than in any other part of the world.

Farm workers in China. Asia has a wealth of natural resources, including fertile farmlands, rich mineral deposits, and vast forests. However, the people in most Asian countries have not used these resources as fully as they might. You may wish to do research to discover why this is so.

A continent of poorly used riches. Some parts of Asia are endowed with vast natural wealth. Almost three fourths of the earth's coal and about two thirds of its petroleum reserves are located on this continent. More than half the tin and tungsten mined in the world each year comes from Asia. In addition, Asia has large forests and many rushing rivers that could be used to produce hy-

droelectricity. Much of Asia is too mountainous, cold, or infertile for farming, but there are good farmlands here also.

Although Asia has many natural resources, most countries here are very poor. The people of these countries have not used their resources as well as they could to achieve a high standard of living. Few Asian nations have developed modern industries, which would help them make better use of their resources.

The home of about six tenths of the world's people. In a continent so large and so rich in natural resources as Asia, you would expect to find many people. The map on pages xii and xiii shows that this assumption is correct. About six tenths of the world's people live in Asia. They are divided into a great many tribes and nationalities that differ in language, customs, and religion.

All parts of Asia are not equally crowded. As the map on pages xii and xiii shows, a large part of the continent has almost no inhabitants. Other parts are densely populated. The map on pages vi and vii and the map below will help to explain this uneven distribution.

The amount of rainfall differs from place to place in Asia. In what ways does rainfall help determine where people live? What other factors affect population distribution? You may wish to do research in other sources before answering these questions.

WORLD AVERAGE ANNUAL PRECIPITATION

Inches

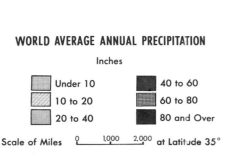

Under 10	40 to 60
10 to 20	60 to 80
20 to 40	80 and Over

Scale of Miles 0   1,000   2,000 at Latitude 35°

Shoppers in Tokyo, Japan. About six tenths of the world's people live in Asia. Most of them are in South and East Asia. Why are these two areas so heavily populated?

WORLD POPULATION

About 3.7 billion people live in the world today. If all these people were evenly distributed over the earth, there would be about sixty-four people to each square mile of land. The map at right shows that this is not the case, however. Some areas are very crowded, and others are almost empty. The three most heavily populated parts of the world are East Asia, South Asia, and Europe. All three are located on the landmass of Eurasia or on the islands nearby. All three areas also have land and climate suited to farming.

World population has more than doubled in the last hundred years. Medical advances, increased food supplies, and improvements in sanitation help to explain this increase. Death rates have fallen in most areas, while birthrates have remained high.

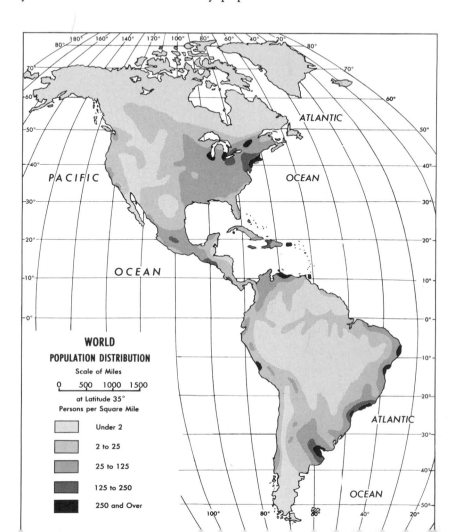

WORLD POPULATION DISTRIBUTION

Scale of Miles

0   500   1000 1500

at Latitude 35°

Persons per Square Mile

Under 2

2 to 25

25 to 125

125 to 250

250 and Over

The population of the world is still expanding. At the present time, the rate of increase is about 2.0 percent annually. If this rate of growth continues, it is estimated that world population will double within thirty years.

In general, the population of the underdeveloped* parts of the world is increasing more rapidly than the population of the industrialized parts. For example, the number of people in Japan increased at a yearly rate of 1.1 percent from 1963 to 1969. During these same years, the annual rate of population increase in South Vietnam was 2.6 percent.

The rapidly expanding population of the world presents one of the greatest challenges facing mankind. Although the world's food supply can be greatly increased, it is probably not unlimited. Many scholars believe that the present rate of population growth must decrease if we are to have a world in which all people have an opportunity to meet their needs.

*See Glossary

Population distribution. The world's population is increasing at an average rate of 2.0 percent each year. What facts help explain this increase? Which areas have the most rapid population growth?

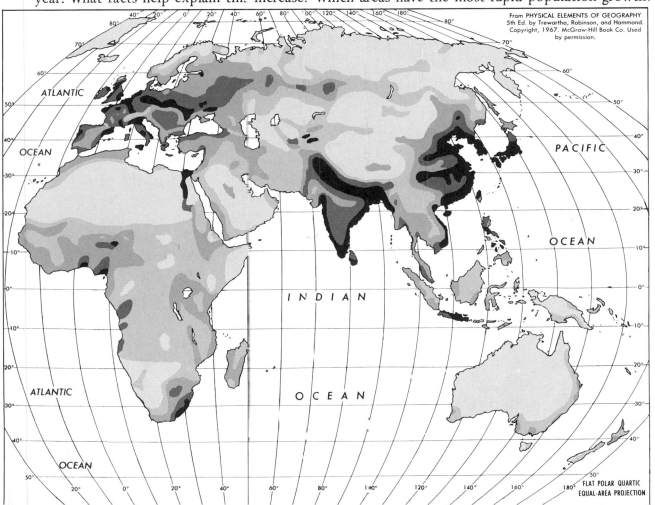

From PHYSICAL ELEMENTS OF GEOGRAPHY 5th Ed. by Trewartha, Robinson, and Hammond. Copyright, 1967. McGraw-Hill Book Co. Used by permission.

FLAT POLAR QUARTIC EQUAL-AREA PROJECTION

A continent of many newly independent nations. Since such a large part of the world's population lives in Asia, you might think that the countries of this continent would have an important voice in world affairs. Until recently, however, this has not been true. One reason is that until the twentieth century the people in many parts of Asia put the interests of their own small tribe or nationality first. As a result, they did not form unified nations that were strong enough to defend themselves. In addition, Asia was industrially behind the nations of the Western world. These weaknesses made it possible for strong European nations to take over large parts of Asia. (See map below.)

Foreign control in most of Asia ended after World War II. During this war, a new feeling that had been arising in the hearts of many Asiatic people became very strong. This feeling was nationalism, the desire to form politically

ASIA IN 1910

The map at left shows the areas of Asia that were independent in 1910 and the areas that were under colonial rule. Several countries shown as independent were under the influence of stronger powers, however. For example, the great Chinese Empire had been forced to sign treaties that gave foreigners control of several of its ports. During and after World War I and World War II, many changes took place in Asia. You may wish to make maps similar to this one in which you show Asia in 1920, in 1940, in 1950, and today. Refer to pages 12-14 of the Skills Manual for help in finding the information you need.

An Independence Day celebration in Indonesia. Since World War II, many countries in Asia have become independent. What is the main reason for this? How did Indonesia gain its independence?

unified, independent countries of their own. In the years after the war, nationalism helped the people in most parts of Asia to achieve independence.

For an example of how nationalism arose in Asia, let us look briefly at the history of Indonesia, a country in Southeast Asia. Before this group of islands was taken over by the Dutch in the eighteenth century, it was divided into many quarreling states. The Dutch, however, brought the people of these states together under a strong colonial government. Roads, railroads, and a shipping line were established, bringing

the people into closer contact with each other. Some Indonesians had an opportunity to attend Western schools, where they learned new ideas about government and the rights of man. They also came to see that colonialism brought greater benefits to people in the ruling Western nations than to the people under colonial rule. Perhaps one of the most important effects of Dutch rule was that it gave all the people of Indonesia something on which to agree. They all wanted to be free from Western rule. All of these factors helped the growth of nationalism in Indonesia. When World

War II ended, the Indonesians refused to live under foreign rule any longer. They fought hard for their independence and won it.

A continent of rising expectations. Nationalism is not the only new feeling in Asia. In addition to demanding independence, many of Asia's people are beginning to demand a greater share of the good things that people in Western industrialized nations have. For many years, most people in Asia took their poverty for granted. They did not know that there was any other way to live. Travel, trade, and communications have increased so much in recent years, however, that this is no longer true. In movies and foreign magazines the people of Asia see pictures of cars, washing machines, and other products commonly used in Western countries such as the United States. What they see is making them realize that people in other parts of the world have a much easier, more comfortable way of life than they do. They want this way of life for themselves. Because Asia's people are beginning to expect more, we say that they are going through a "revolution of rising expectations."

The rising expectations of Asia's people are making them dissatisfied and restless. Many people thought that independence would solve their problems. However, becoming independent did not suddenly create the factories, schools, hospitals, or other institutions needed to bring the better way of life they wanted. As you do research about Southeast Asia, you may wish to discover some of the reasons why it has been difficult for the people there to solve their problems and fulfill their rising expectations. You may also wish to discover what progress they have made in solving their problems.

Chinese farm workers harvesting grain. Most of Asia's people earn their living by farming. They live in villages and are generally very poor. In the past, Asians took their poverty for granted, but today they are going through a "revolution of rising expectations." What does this mean?

SOUTHEAST ASIA

An Overview of Southeast Asia

In the southeastern part of Asia are two peninsulas and many islands. These form the region called Southeast Asia. (See the picture of a globe on page 1.) In the northwestern part of this region is the Indo-Chinese Peninsula, which extends off the mainland of Asia. Stretching southward from this peninsula is a long, narrow body of land called the Malay Peninsula. (See map below.) To the south and east are the islands of Indonesia and the Philippines. Together, the islands and peninsulas of Southeast Asia form a land area that is about half the size of the United States.

Southeast Asia is a treasure-house of natural resources. Southeast Asia's many natural resources make it one of the world's important regions. Its farmlands produce more rice for export than any

Southeast Asia is made up of two large peninsulas and many islands. The picture at right shows an island off the tip of the Malay Peninsula. What is the name of the other large peninsula in Southeast Asia? What are the names of the two main groups of islands in this region? What country or countries lie in each of the geographical divisions shown on this map? (Compare this map with the map on pages 8 and 9.)

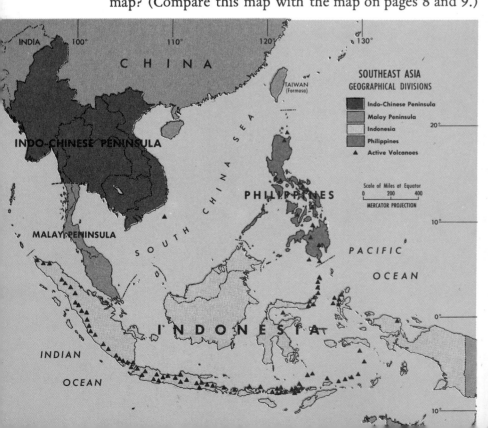

SOUTHEAST ASIA
GEOGRAPHICAL DIVISIONS

- Indo-Chinese Peninsula
- Malay Peninsula
- Indonesia
- Philippines
- ▲ Active Volcanoes

Scale of Miles at Equator
0   200   400
MERCATOR PROJECTION

INDIA 100°   CHINA   110°   120°   130°

TAIWAN (Formosa)

INDO-CHINESE PENINSULA

SOUTH CHINA SEA

PHILIPPINES

MALAY PENINSULA

PACIFIC OCEAN

INDONESIA

INDIAN OCEAN

Cultivating a rice field in Indonesia. Rice is the chief food eaten by the people of Southeast Asia. In addition, this region exports large quantities of rice to other parts of the world. The export of rice is very important to Southeast Asia's people. Why do you suppose this is so?

other part of the world. Three fourths of the world's copra, more than four fifths of its natural rubber, and almost half of its tin come from this region. In addition, Southeast Asia is the most important petroleum-producing area in the eastern part of Asia.

Important travel routes pass through Southeast Asia. Southeast Asia's location also makes it important. Much of this region lies near the shortest water route between Europe and the eastern part of Asia. Each year, thousands of ships travel through the Strait of Malacca, west of Malaya, and the narrow sea passages between the islands of Indo-

nesia. (See the map on pages 8 and 9.) Southeast Asia is also an important stopping-off place on around-the-world air routes.

There are many newly independent nations in Southeast Asia. Before World War II, there was only one independent nation in Southeast Asia. This was Siam, now called Thailand. All of the other countries in Southeast Asia except the Philippines were controlled by nations in Europe. The Philippines was controlled by the United States.

Today, almost all of Southeast Asia has gained independence. The independent countries in this region are Burma,

Cambodia, Laos, Thailand North and South Vietnam, the Philippines, Indonesia, Malaysia, and Singapore. (See the map on pages 8 and 9.)

Only a few parts of Southeast Asia are still controlled by outsiders. Brunei, on the island of Borneo,* was scheduled to become a part of Malaysia. It chose not to, however, and is still under British protection. Parts of the island of Timor are under Portuguese control.

The countries of Southeast Asia differ from one another in important ways. Some are large and others are small. In a few nations, the governments are fairly democratic, but in others, the people have almost no opportunity to decide how they should be governed. One country, North Vietnam, has a Communist government. The languages that the people speak and most of the customs they follow also differ from country to country.

In other ways the countries of Southeast Asia are much alike. Their land, their climate, and the ways in which their people make a living have many similarities. Each independent country here is also determined to guard its freedom and make its own decisions.

The nations of Southeast Asia have many of the same problems, also. Except for Thailand, these nations have little experience in self-government. They do not have enough roads, railroads, schools, hospitals, or industries. In addition, all of these nations must import many of their manufactured goods and pay for them by exporting raw materials from mines, forests, and farms.

Southeast Asia's people are our neighbors. Southeast Asia is the home of about 290 million people. Although they live far away from us, these people are our global neighbors. They produce things we need, and we furnish them with things they need. We can give them support in solving many of their problems, and they can make our own lives richer and more interesting by sharing with us their art and many of their ideas.

In order to cooperate most successfully with Southeast Asia's people, we need to understand them. The following chapters provide many opportunities for you to make discoveries about life in this important region of the world.

*See Glossary

Rice fields at the foot of Mount Mayon, an active volcano in the Philippines. The farmlands shown in this picture are very fertile. You may wish to do research about volcanoes to discover why this is so.

Part 1
Land and Climate

Imagine that you have just returned home after spending a year in Southeast Asia. While you were there, you had opportunities to travel through many parts of this region. A newspaper has asked you to write an article describing your travels, including information about the following:

- the countries you visited
- the main land and water features you saw in each country
- the weather in various parts of Southeast Asia at different times of the year
- ways in which land and water features and climate affected the everyday lives of the people you met

Prepare an article based on these topics. The pictures and text in Part 1 and in other parts of this book provide much of the information you will need. Refer to pages 12-14 of the Skills Manual for help in finding information in other sources.

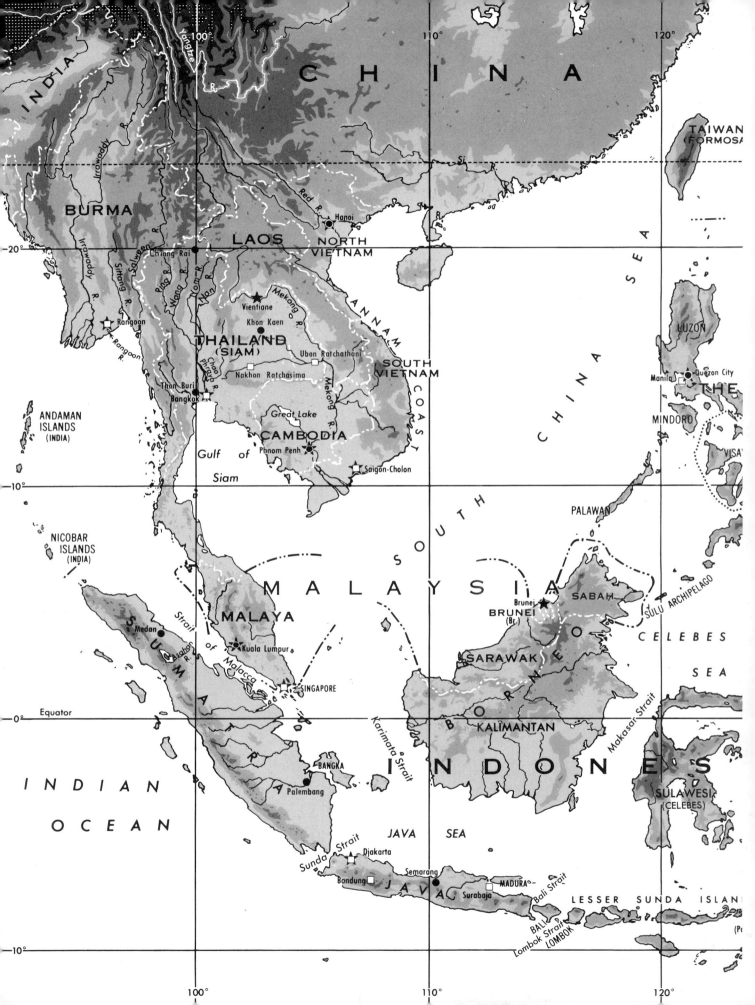

SOUTHEAST ASIA

Cities
- ◐ 500,000 to 1,000,000
- ☐ 1,000,000 and Over
- ★ Capitals

Elevations in Feet

	15,000 and Over
	10,000 to 15,000
	5,000 to 10,000
	1,000 to 5,000
	0 to 1,000

Scale of Miles at Equator
0   100   200   300   400
MERCATOR PROJECTION

RYUKYU ISLANDS (JAPAN)

------ Tropic of Cancer ------

PHILIPPINES

‹YAS

‹MINDANAO

P A C I F I C

O C E A N

I   A

M A L U K U
(MOLUCCAS)

WEST IRIAN
(WEST NEW GUINEA)

B A N D A
S E A

A R A F U R A
S E A

D S

★ Dili
(Port.)

ort.)

TIMOR

T I M O R   S E A

130°   140°

1 Land

Mountain ranges and seas help to divide Southeast Asia into many isolated parts. Some of the seas are connected with the great Pacific Ocean. Others are arms of the Indian Ocean. Along some of the seacoasts are lowlands that are densely populated. Many of the river plains between the mountain ranges are also densely populated.

Let's take an imaginary spaceship journey over Southeast Asia to learn more about the geography of this region. First we shall examine the Indo-Chinese Peninsula, where the countries of Laos, Cambodia, and North and South Vietnam are located. Most of Burma and Thailand are also located on this peninsula. (Compare map at left with the one on page 2.)

The Indo-Chinese Peninsula

Mountains of the Indo-Chinese Peninsula. We see many mountains as we look down on the Indo-Chinese Peninsula. (See map at left.) In the north are high ranges that separate most of the peninsula from the rest of Asia. Extending southward from these barriers are several other ranges. They reach through the Indo-Chinese Peninsula like giant fingers, and stretch on into the sea. In

Southeast Asia is a region of rugged highlands and fertile plains. Where are the largest lowland areas located? the highest mountains?

comparison with some of the mountains of India and China, these are quite low. Most of them rise less than 9,000 feet above sea level. Nearly all of these mountain chains are highest in the north. The peninsula's highest point is a mountain peak in northern Burma. This peak rises 19,296 feet above sea level.

As we fly over the mountains, we see forests below us. The forests are very thick on the ranges that stretch along the edges of the peninsula, for the rainfall here is heaviest. On the central highlands that receive less rain, the forests are not so dense. Some of these slopes are covered with savannas, which are grasslands dotted with trees.

Lowlands of the Indo-Chinese Peninsula. Several great river valleys are located between the mountain ranges of the Indo-Chinese Peninsula. In the western part of the peninsula is the valley

The countryside near Bangkok, Thailand. Several great river valleys cut between the mountain ranges of the Indo-Chinese Peninsula. In which of these valleys do you think this picture might have been taken?

of the Irrawaddy River. (See the map on pages 8 and 9.) This river begins in the mountains on Burma's northern border and flows southward to the sea. As we look southeastward from the Irrawaddy, we see the valley of the Chao Phraya in Thailand. Farther east is the mighty Mekong River. It forms much of the border between Thailand and Laos, and then flows across Cambodia and South Vietnam. In the northeastern part of the Indo-Chinese Peninsula is the Red River of North Vietnam.

Where the large rivers of the Indo-Chinese Peninsula flow into the sea, there are plains called deltas. These deltas are formed mostly of sand and silt carried here by the rivers from the land through which they flow. The delta of the Red River is one of the most densely populated parts of Southeast Asia. Some of the other deltas, such as the Irrawaddy Delta, were largely covered with swamps until one hundred years ago. Today many of the swamps have been drained for rice farms.

Several of Southeast Asia's important cities are located on the deltas of the Indo-Chinese Peninsula. Among these are Rangoon in Burma, Bangkok in Thailand, Saigon and its suburb Cholon in South Vietnam, and Hanoi in North Vietnam.

The Great Lake. There is only one large lake on the Indo-Chinese Peninsula. This is the Great Lake or Tonle Sap, in the central lowland of Cambodia. (See map on pages 8 and 9.) The Great Lake was once an inlet of the sea. Over

A Problem To Solve
How do the land and water features of Southeast Asia affect the people? In forming hypotheses to solve this problem, you will need to consider how land and water features affect:
1. ways of earning a living in Southeast Asia
2. transportation and communication in this region
3. where the people of Southeast Asia live
Other chapters of this book provide additional information that will be helpful in solving this problem. Use the Index to locate the information you need.

See Skills Manual, pages 2-4

the centuries, however, the mouth of this inlet has been filled in with silt deposited by the Mekong River.

The Malay Peninsula and Singapore

From our spaceship we now look southward to the Malay Peninsula. The northern part of this peninsula is included in the countries of Thailand and Burma. The southern part is occupied by Malaya.[*]

Mountains and valleys of the Malay Peninsula. Several ranges of forested mountains extend from north to south through the Malay Peninsula. (See maps on pages 2 and 8.) In many places, short rivers have carved valleys through the highlands. Most of these interior river lowlands are covered with swamps or dense, green rainforests.

Coastal lowlands of the Malay Peninsula. Bordering the mountains of the Malay Peninsula are coastal lowlands. Some of these lowlands are covered with swampy forests. Others have been cleared for farming. In Chapter 10 we will learn about the rubber plantations on the western coastal lowlands of the peninsula.

The island of Singapore. Off the southern coast of the Malay Peninsula is the tiny island of Singapore. It is connected to the peninsula by a causeway. One of the world's busiest port cities, also called Singapore, is located on this island. Outside the city are suburbs and many little farms. There are also scattered patches of swamps and forests.

The island of Singapore is located off the southern coast of the Malay Peninsula.

*See Glossary

Indonesia

South and east of the Malay Peninsula are islands that belong to the great archipelago* of Indonesia. Altogether there are about three thousand islands in this archipelago. Most of them are very small. Five, however, are among the largest islands in the world. These are Borneo, Sumatra, Java, Sulawesi, and New Guinea.

The Indonesian archipelago is divided mainly between the independent nations of Indonesia and Malaysia. (Compare the map on page 2 with the map on pages 8 and 9.) Two areas, however, are under Western* control. These are Portuguese Timor and Brunei. The western part of the island of New Guinea was formerly under United Nations administration, but is now a province of Indonesia. It is known as West Irian. The eastern part of New Guinea, administered by Australia, is not commonly considered part of Asia.

As we study this archipelago from our spaceship, we notice that the seas and straits separating Sumatra, Java, Borneo, and the Malay Peninsula are light blue. This indicates that the water here is shallow. Scientists say that at times long ago there was less water in the seas than there is now, and these shallow areas were above water. During these periods, the Malay Peninsula and the western islands of Indonesia were connected by land. Boats were not needed to transport animals, plants, or people from the mainland of Asia to these islands. Today, many of the plants and animals in this part of Indonesia are like those on the mainland of Asia. Tigers and elephants roam in the forests of Sumatra, as they do in India.

In the easternmost islands of Indonesia, however, there are marsupials* like the ones on the neighboring continent of Australia. When the seas were lower, the straits that separated some of these islands from Australia were narrow enough to swim across. Other islands were connected to Australia by land bridges, over which animals could easily travel.

The island of Java. The most important island in the country of Indonesia is Java. (See map on page 8.) Although

Prehistoric land bridges. Scientists believe that land bridges once connected parts of Southeast Asia that are now separated by water.
1. What are some facts that help support this theory?
2. Compare this map with the map on pages 8 and 9. What parts of Southeast Asia were once connected by land bridges?

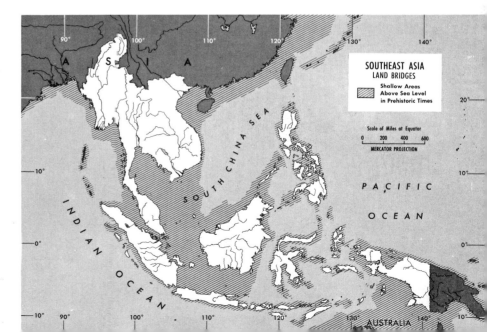

Sumatra is one of the five main islands in the archipelago of Indonesia. What are the other four? What land features would you see on a trip through these five islands?

it is the smallest of the main islands, nearly two thirds of the country's people live here. The volcanoes that stretch from east to west through the island help to explain why. Long ago, people discovered that ashes and other materials from the volcanoes helped to make the soil here very good for growing crops. There are about eighty-five volcanoes on Java, and seventeen are still active. Millions of people live on Java's fertile mountain slopes. Many others live on the coastal lowlands that border the mountains.

The island of Sumatra. Northwest of Java is Sumatra, the second most

There are coastal lowlands on both sides of Sumatra's mountain backbone. On the west coast, the lowlands are very narrow, but along the east coast they are wide. Until recently, the dense, swampy forests that cover much of the eastern coastal lowlands discouraged most people from living there. Today, however, some of Southeast Asia's most productive farms, plantations, and oil fields are located on these lowlands.

The island of Borneo. East of Sumatra is the huge island of Borneo. Part of this island is a British protectorate and parts are included in the countries of Malaysia and Indonesia. (See map on pages 8-9.)

Far fewer people live on Borneo than on Java or Sumatra. The reasons for this are due partly to Borneo's geography. A major part of this mountainous island is covered with dense rainforests or swamps. In addition, the heavy rains that fall throughout the year in most of Borneo wash out of the soil the minerals and other substances needed to grow crops. Only a small part of the land is now under cultivation, but more is being cleared for farming all the time. As a comparison of the maps on pages 85 and 8-9 shows, the main farming areas are in the coastal lowlands.

The island of Sulawesi. East of Borneo is Sulawesi, which was formerly called Celebes. As we examine Sulawesi, we notice that it resembles an octopus with arms reaching out in four directions. (See map on page 135.) Curving, underwater mountain ranges thrust their peaks above the sea to form this strangely shaped island. There are many beautiful waterfalls and lakes on Sulawesi. Green rainforests cover most

important island of Indonesia. (See map on pages 8-9.) A belt of green mountains forms a backbone along the west side of the island. Many of them were formed by volcanoes. Scattered among the mountains are fertile basins and river valleys where the land has been cleared for farming.

of the land. Most of the people on Sulawesi live on the northeastern and southwestern tips of the island, where there is fertile volcanic soil.

West Irian. East of Sulawesi is New Guinea, the second largest island in the world. Only the western part of this island, called West Irian, is considered a part of Southeast Asia. A very high range of mountains extends from east to west through central West Irian. There are other highlands north of this range. The land south of the central range is generally level. Swamps and thick forests cover this broad lowland.

Others islands of Indonesia. Between New Guinea, Sulawesi, and Java are hundreds of smaller islands. Some belong to a group called the Lesser Sunda Islands. (See the map on pages 8 and 9.) Others belong to a group called the Maluku.* Many of these small islands in eastern Indonesia are the peaks of underwater volcanoes.

The Philippines

Now our spaceship is flying across the Philippines. This cluster of islands does not spread over as wide an area as Indonesia. (See the map on pages 8 and 9.) There are about 7,100 islands in the Philippines, but only eleven are big enough to be important. At the northern end is the largest island, Luzon. At the southern end is the second largest island, Mindanao. Between Luzon and Mindanao is an important island group called the Visayas. Somewhat separated from all these islands and stretching southwestward toward Borneo are the Sulu Archipelago and long, narrow Palawan Island.

Mountains of the Philippines. As we study the islands of the Philippines from our spaceship, we see that they are very rugged. The smaller islands are the peaks of underwater mountains. Curving through the large islands are mountain ranges that run in several different directions. The ranges that stretch through Luzon and Mindanao run generally north and south. In Palawan, however, the mountains are part of the same range that stretches southwestward through Borneo. As in Indonesia,

16

there are many volcanoes in the Philippines. Most of the mountain slopes on these islands are forested. In some places where the forests have burned, there are large grasslands or bamboo thickets.

Lowlands of the Philippines. Though the islands of the Philippines are mainly covered with mountains, we see several important lowlands. In northern Luzon is the fertile valley of the Cagayan River. Southwest of this lowland is the large central plain of Luzon where Manila, the most important city in the Philippines, is located. There are many farms on both of these lowlands. On the island of Mindanao there are two large river valleys and several narrow coastal plains. Much of Mindanao is covered with forests. In the past, only a small part of this island was used for farming. However, more and more land is being cleared all the time.

Most of the other main islands of the Philippines have central mountains that are ringed with coastal lowlands. Some of these lowlands are very densely populated. In later chapters we will learn how the people here and in other parts of Southeast Asia live and work.

Luzon is the largest island in the Philippines. Although this island country is very mountainous, it has several good farming areas. Compare the maps on pages 85 and 133. Where are the main farming areas of the Philippines located? What facts help to explain why this is so?

On the island of **Borneo**. In most parts of Southeast Asia, the climate is warm and rainy. Palm trees are typical of the vegetation that grows along the coasts of this region.

2 Climate

Dense forests of tall trees and climbing vines cover much of Southeast Asia. In most of this region the air is very humid and the rainfall is heavy. The temperature does not change much from summer to winter anywhere except in the far north.

Why most of Southeast Asia is warm throughout the year. If we look at the countries of Southeast Asia on a globe, it will help us to understand why most of this region does not have cold win-

ters. All but the far northern part is close to the equator.

The part of the earth near the equator is not tipped far away from the sun in winter the way lands nearer the North and South poles are. For this reason, it receives warm sunshine all year long, and the temperature does not change very much from one season to another.

Highlands are cooler than lowlands. The only places we find cool weather

Physical Needs

See pages 141-142

A Problem To Solve

Most of Southeast Asia has a warm climate. How does the climate of this region affect the ways in which people meet their needs for food, clothing, and shelter? The pictures and text in Chapters 6 and 10 provide additional information that will be useful in solving this problem.

See Skills Manual, pages 2-4

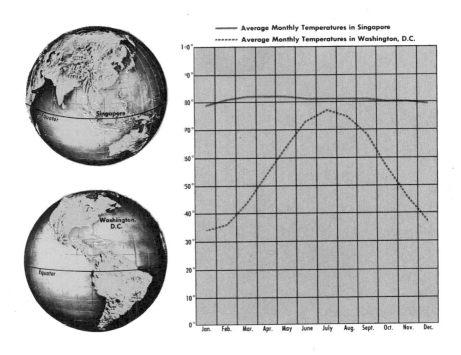

Average Monthly Temperatures in Singapore
Average Monthly Temperatures in Washington, D.C.

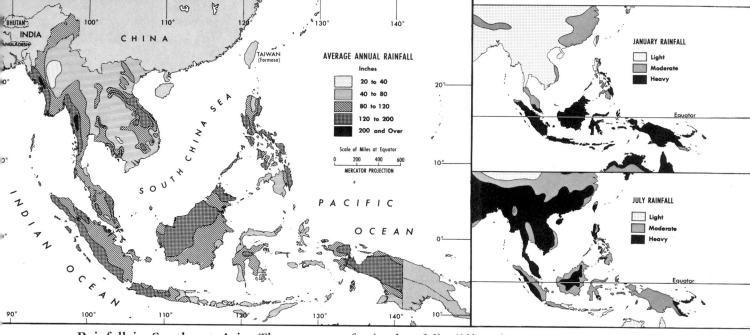

AVERAGE ANNUAL RAINFALL

Inches

20 to 40
40 to 80
80 to 120
120 to 200
200 and Over

Scale of Miles at Equator
0   200   400   600
MERCATOR PROJECTION

JANUARY RAINFALL
Light
Moderate
Heavy

JULY RAINFALL
Light
Moderate
Heavy

Rainfall in Southeast Asia. The amount of rain that falls differs from season to season in much of Southeast Asia. Why is this so? Which parts of this region receive the most rainfall each year? Which receive the least? (Compare these maps with the map on pages 8 and 9.)

close to the equator are in the high mountains. Far above sea level, the air is thin and does not hold the warmth of the sun. Some people in Southeast Asia travel to the highlands when they wish to escape the heat.

Rainfall differs from season to season in much of Southeast Asia. Though the temperature does not change much throughout the year in most of Southeast Asia, the amount of rainfall does. In many places, the year is divided into a rainy season and a dry season. Let's learn about these seasons.

The Climate of the Indo-Chinese Peninsula

Summer is the wet season and winter is the dry season in most of the Indo-Chinese Peninsula. It is a rainy day in July, and we are driving along a road in southern Burma. This is one of the countries on the Indo-Chinese Peninsula. The countryside looks green and

the streams are flooded, for it has rained frequently since May. Summer is the rainy season in this area. In some places the rain comes every day. Warm, moist ocean winds from the southwest help to bring this rainfall. These winds, which blow only in summer, are called the summer monsoons.

It is October now, and the rains are becoming less frequent. Soon they will stop almost entirely, for winter is the dry season here. During the first part of the dry season the weather is cool. In February, however, it becomes unpleasantly hot. The countryside is dusty and brown, trees are bare, and many streams are dry.

The winds that blow during the dry season come mainly from across the seas to the northeast. When they reach the Indo-Chinese Peninsula, they are forced to rise in order to cross highlands along the Annam coast. This causes the winds to cool, which in turn causes some of their moisture to condense and fall as rain. By the time the winds have crossed the highlands, they have become drier. Also, when they move down the other side of the highlands, they become warmer. Instead of giving off

A rainy day in Burma. Most of the Indo-Chinese Peninsula receives heavy rainfall from May to October. Winter is the dry season here. How do these rainfall patterns affect farming in this area?

moisture, they absorb it from the land. This is one reason why the land west of these highlands is dry during this season. By comparing the map on pages 8-9 with the top right-hand map on page 20, you can see that the Annam coast receives moderate rainfall during the dry season, but in the rest of the Indo-Chinese Peninsula the rainfall is light.

The pattern of rainfall greatly influences farming on the Indo-Chinese Peninsula. People depend on the summer

A beach at Nha Trang, South Vietnam. In much of the Indo-Chinese Peninsula, winter weather is warm enough for people to go to the beach. Rainfall is generally light at this time of the year.

monsoon rains for water to flood their rice fields. When the rains are late or too little rain comes, crops may fail. The people often hold elaborate ceremonies to encourage the rainy season when it is delayed.

Some parts of the Indo-Chinese Peninsula are drier than others. The large map on page 20 shows us that some parts of the Indo-Chinese Peninsula receive less rainfall than others. One of these drier areas is in the central lowlands of Burma. When we travel to this dry area we see farmers working in fields of millet, cotton, and other crops. There are no dense forests here. The hillsides are covered with coarse grass, thorny bushes, and clumps of trees.

The map on pages 8-9 will help to explain why some parts of the Indo-Chinese Peninsula receive less rainfall than others. When we compare this map with the large map on page 20, we see that the places with the lightest rainfall are bordered by highlands. The highlands shelter these drier regions from moisture-filled winds.

The Climate of the Malay Peninsula and Indonesia

Most of Indonesia and the Malay Peninsula receive some rain every month of the year. Now we are walking through a rubber plantation in Malaya. (See map on pages 8-9.) On either side of us are rows of tall rubber trees with glossy, dark-green leaves. These trees grow best in warm regions where rain falls throughout the year. Most of the Malay Peninsula and Indonesia have this kind of climate. In parts of these two areas the air is often calm and uncomfortable. Thunderstorms occur almost every day.

In much of Indonesia and the Malay Peninsula more rain falls in some seasons than in others. (See small maps on page 20.) These seasons of especially heavy rainfall differ from place to place. In the southeastern islands of Indonesia, there is also a season when almost no rain falls.

The Climate of the Philippines

When we travel through the Philippines we find that the weather is quite warm everywhere except in the mountains. Rainfall differs from place to place in the Philippines. As in Indonesia, all parts of the country do not have a rainy season at the same time. Much of the northwestern part of the Philippines has dry winters and springs, and wet summers and autumns. In much of the southeastern part rain falls all year long, but the months of December, January, and February are rainiest. Other sections of the country have heavy rain the year round.

Typhoons. During our visit to the Philippines, there is a terrible storm called a typhoon. Typhoons are like the hurricanes that sometimes strike parts of the United States. They occur most often between August and November. When a typhoon arrives, howling winds and sheets of blinding rain sink fishing boats in the harbors and flatten crops in the fields.

Though typhoons are most frequent in northern Luzon, they also strike the central islands. The island of Mindanao, in the southern part of the country, is seldom hit by these destructive storms.

In the Philippines, the weather is warm everywhere except in areas high above sea level. Why is the weather cooler in these areas?

Explore Volcanoes

Many mountains in Southeast Asia were formed by volcanic eruptions. Do research and prepare an oral report about volcanoes. In your report, include information about the following:

1. how a volcano is formed
2. harmful effects of volcanic eruptions
3. ways in which volcanoes can be helpful
4. the relationship between earthquakes and volcanoes
5. the Pacific "ring of fire"
6. some of the world's famous volcanoes

You may also wish to explain why you would, or would not, like to live near a volcano. Refer to pages 12-17 of the Skills Manual for help in locating information and preparing an interesting report.

Typhoons

Typhoons, which sometimes strike the Philippines, also occur in other parts of Asia. Do research and prepare a report about these destructive storms. In your report, include information about the following:

1. what a typhoon is, and how it forms
2. the parts of the world where typhoons occur and the times of the year when they are most likely to form
3. some of the most destructive typhoons in history
4. a description of what happens when a typhoon strikes

Use Your Creativity

In the tropical seas that border Southeast Asia are many reefs and tiny islands formed of coral. Do research to find answers to the following questions about coral.

1. What is coral?
2. How are coral islands and reefs formed?
3. What do some of the different kinds of coral look like? (Try to find pictures or samples of coral.)

Then imagine that you have gone skin diving off an island in Southeast Asia to observe coral formations. Draw pictures of the kinds of coral you saw. (You might like to include tropical fish in your pictures.) Be sure to color your drawings. Then show your pictures to your classmates and explain to them what you have discovered about coral.

Investigate Drifting Continents

Some scientists believe that all the continents of the world were once very close together and may have formed one or two giant continents. According to their theory, called the theory of continental drift, these landmasses slowly drifted apart. Do research about the theory of continental drift to discover answers to the following questions.

1. Who was Alfred Wegener? What were his beliefs concerning continental drift?
2. According to some scientists today, what caused the landmasses to drift apart?
3. What evidence have scientists gathered to support the theory of continental drift?
4. Why do some scientists dispute the theory of continental drift?

As you do your research, you may think of other questions you want to explore. Then summarize your findings in an oral report. You may wish to make outline maps to illustrate the theory of continental drift.

Thinking Together

As a class, discuss the following question. How do mountains affect the ways people live and work? To prepare for the discussion, do research about mountainous areas in Southeast Asia and in other parts of the world. For example, you may wish to find out how mountains affect people in South America, Switzerland, China, and Japan. The following questions will guide your research.

1. How do mountains affect:
   a. where people live
   b. ways in which people earn their living
   c. transportation and communication
2. What kinds of natural resources are often found in mountainous areas?
3. In what ways, if any, can mountain barriers be helpful to people?

Part 2

History and Government

During the past two thousand years, traders, colonial officials, missionaries, and immigrants from other countries have brought many ideas and customs to Southeast Asia.

How have people from other lands influenced life in Southeast Asia?

The chapters in Part 2 provide information that will help you solve this problem. In forming your hypotheses,* consider how foreign influences have affected the following:

- religious practices in Southeast Asia
- government in Southeast Asia
- the lives of the people in large cities of this region
- the arts of Southeast Asia
- festivals and recreation in this region
- ways of earning a living in Southeast Asia

The chapters in Parts 3 and 4 provide additional information that will be useful in testing your hypotheses.

*See Skills Manual, pages 2-4

Buddhist monks at the ruins of Angkor Wat, in Cambodia. This great temple was built by the Khmers in the twelfth century. You may wish to do research about the Khmers and their empire.

This carving from the Buddhist temple at Borobudur, on Java, shows traders from India sailing to Southeast Asia. These merchants began traveling to the island of Java about two thousand years ago. Why do you think they came here? Do you think such a voyage would have been easy? Why? Why not?

3 Southeast Asia Long Ago

Early people of Southeast Asia. Long before Christ was born, tribesmen from the neighboring lands of Tibet, China, and India traveled into the green valleys of the Indo-Chinese Peninsula. Some of their descendants journeyed still farther to the Malay Peninsula and to the islands of Southeast Asia. Most of the newcomers had light-brown skin, and eyes that appeared to be somewhat slanted. They knew how to make better tools and weapons than the small, dark-skinned people already living in Southeast Asia. Some of these dark-skinned people were pushed back into the remote mountains and jungles. Others stayed in the valleys and coastal plains, intermarrying with the newcomers. As time went on, more and more settlers arrived, bringing new ideas and skills.

By the first century A.D., there were many different groups of people living in Southeast Asia. Some groups in the remote regions gathered roots and other food, or hunted. Others burned trees in the forests to clear land for farming. When the soil in these clearings was no longer fertile, they moved on and cleared new land. The people in the coastal lowlands and river valleys grew rice in

flooded fields. They knew how to make tools and weapons out of metal, and build boats strong enough to sail long distances across the seas.

Traders traveling between China and India visit Southeast Asia. In addition to the settlers who came overland, Southeast Asia had visitors who came by sea. The map on pages vi and vii will help explain why. This region is located on the water route between India and China. Traders traveling between these two lands stopped in Southeast Asia. Seamen from Southeast Asia also sailed to India and China.

Southeast Asians learn new ways from the Indians. Some of the Indian traders established trading settlements in Southeast Asia. Later, religious leaders and other people from India also settled in these towns. From the Indians, people in many parts of Southeast Asia learned about the Hindu and Buddhist

A Problem To Solve

Long before the birth of Christ, tribesmen from Tibet, China, and India migrated from their homelands to Southeast Asia. The arrows on the map at right show the routes they followed. Throughout history, Southeast Asia has been influenced by people from other lands. Why has this been so? In forming hypotheses to solve this problem, you will need to consider facts about:

1. the location of Southeast Asia
2. resources and products of this region

Chapters 4 and 11 provide additional information.

See Skills Manual, pages 2-4

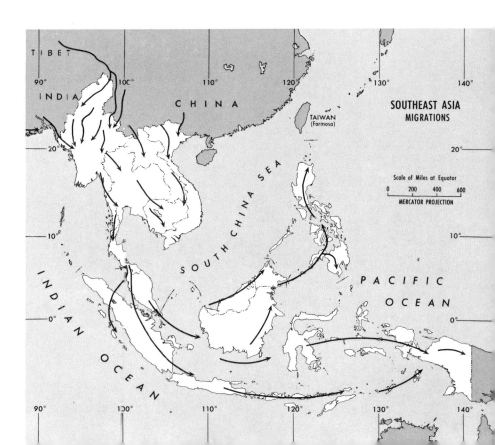

SOUTHEAST ASIA MIGRATIONS

Scale of Miles at Equator
0   200   400   600
MERCATOR PROJECTION

religions. The Indians also brought with them new ideas about government, art, and architecture. Southeast Asians did not copy their Indian teachers exactly. Instead, they often used Indian ideas to create something different of their own.

Kingdoms grow up around Indian trading settlements. Some of the Indian trading settlements grew into powerful cities that gained control of neighboring territories. Kingdoms were established, which fought each other frequently to gain more power and territory. Several

Dancers in Thailand act out an episode from the *Ramayana*, a story-poem that originated in India many hundreds of years ago. How do you think people in Southeast Asia first learned about this story?

A **carved battle scene** showing Khmer warriors fighting neighboring tribesmen. What areas of Southeast Asia did the Khmers control?

kingdoms grew into great empires that at various times controlled large parts of Southeast Asia. Some of these empires were located on the Indo-Chinese Peninsula. Others had their capitals on the islands of Java or Sumatra.

One of the most interesting of these empires was the Khmer Empire, which began as a little kingdom near the Mekong River. During the twelfth and early thirteenth centuries, the Khmer rulers gained control of most of the fertile lowlands on the Indo-Chinese Peninsula. Their empire even included the northern part of the Malay Peninsula.

The Khmer capital was at Angkor, near the Great Lake. (See map on page 125.) Ruins of magnificent stone temples built in this city still stand today. One temple, the Angkor Wat, is among the largest religious buildings in the world. (See picture on pages 26 and 27.)

The Khmers were frequently at war with neighboring tribesmen called the Thai. These tribesmen gradually overran much of the Khmers' territory and in 1431 invaded Angkor. Soon, all that remained of the once-great Khmer Empire was Cambodia.

Some Southeast Asians borrow customs from the Chinese. The Khmers learned many of their customs from the Indians, but there were other people in Southeast Asia whose teachers were the Chinese. These people lived in the territory later known as Vietnam. In 111 B.C. the northern part of this territory became part of the Chinese Empire. It did not regain its independence until A.D. 939. As a result, the people here adopted many Chinese customs. (See Chapter 6.)

The religion of Islam is brought to Southeast Asia. In the fifteenth century the religion of Islam became important in Southeast Asia. For many years before this time, Moslem* traders from Arabia and western India had been coming to Southeast Asia. However, the only place where they had converted large numbers of people was in northern Sumatra. Early in the fifteenth century a trading center was established at Malacca, on the southwestern coast of the Malay Peninsula. Moslem traders persuaded many people in Malacca to accept Islam. From here, this religion spread to other parts of the Malay Peninsula and to the island of Java.

What was Southeast Asia like in the fifteenth century? Let's see what Southeast Asia was like during the fifteenth century, when Islam was becoming impor-
*See Glossary

An ancient Chinese painting shows people from Vietnam and Borneo bringing gifts to the ruler of China. From 111 B.C. to A.D. 939, China ruled the northern part of what is now Vietnam. In what ways did the Chinese influence life in this area? Chapter 6 will help you answer this question.

A mosque in Malaysia. About 100 million people in Malaysia and Indonesia follow the religion of Islam. What facts about the history of these two areas help to explain why this is so?

tant. The ancestors of the present-day Vietnamese people were extending their control down the eastern edge of the Indo-Chinese Peninsula. In the lowlands of the Chao Phraya River, a kingdom later known as Thailand was becoming important. It was bordered on the southeast by Cambodia. The other countries that we find on modern maps of Southeast Asia were divided into numerous little independent territories.

Southeast Asia was an important trading area in the fifteenth century. As we have learned, one reason for this was its location on the water route between India and China. Another reason was that Southeast Asia produced goods that the rest of the world wanted to buy. The desire for some of these products—especially the spices—was to help shape the history of this region in the years to come.

4 Westerners Come to Southeast Asia

Picking pepper on Java. In the 1500's, people from Europe began coming to Southeast Asia to obtain pepper, cloves, and other spices. Why did Europeans want these products?

Exchange

See pages 137-140

In 1498, the Portuguese explorer Vasco da Gama completed the first all-water journey from Europe to India. Why did Portugal want to find an all-water route to this part of the world? Why was the line of demarcation shown on this map established?

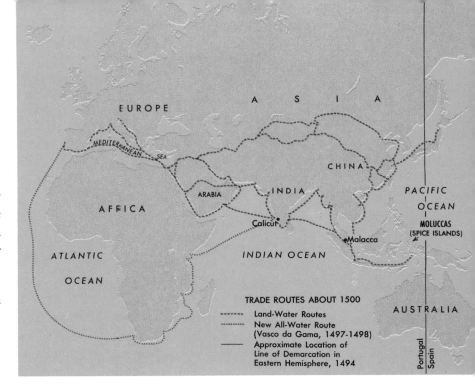

TRADE ROUTES ABOUT 1500
- - - - - Land-Water Routes
· · · · · New All-Water Route (Vasco da Gama, 1497-1498)
————— Approximate Location of Line of Demarcation in Eastern Hemisphere, 1494

Spices help to shape the history of Southeast Asia. Five hundred years ago, spices such as pepper, cloves, and nutmeg were far more important than they are today. There were no refrigerators, and many foods spoiled quickly. Spices helped to preserve food. They also made it taste better when it was no longer fresh. The main spice-producing areas of the world were in Southeast Asia. The eagerness of Europeans to obtain spices and other valuable products from this region helped to shape its history.

Portugal gains control of the spice trade. One day in 1498, a Portuguese explorer named Vasco da Gama sailed into the harbor of Calicut, India. The expedition under his command had just completed the first all-water journey from Europe to India. (See map above.) From India, ships could sail on to the distant spice lands of Southeast Asia.

Da Gama's discovery of an all-water route to the spice lands was very important to Portugal and other countries in Europe. The map above shows that the old trade routes between Europe and the spice lands crossed both land and water. All of these routes were controlled by Arab and Italian merchants. The prices that people in western Europe had to pay for spices and other goods were very high. Therefore, many Europeans wanted to find an all-water route to the spice lands so they could buy the goods directly from merchants there. Portugal had still another reason for seeking a new route to the spice lands. The Arab traders were Moslems—followers of the religion called Islam. Moslems had tried to invade Portugal for many years, and were bitterly hated by the Portuguese.

In order to make as much money as possible, the Portuguese wanted to control the spice trade completely. However, the Moslems already controlled several trading ports in Southeast Asia. In 1511, Portugal captured the most important of these ports, Malacca, on the southwestern coast of the Malay Peninsula. During the years that followed, the Portuguese established fortified posts in Southeast Asia. They patrolled the seas near the spice regions to keep the ships of other nations out. Portugal also tried to spread Christianity in the spice lands. It had little success, however, for most of the Portuguese who came to Southeast Asia behaved like conquerors and made the people there hate them.

Spain claims the Philippines. Portugal was not the only nation that wanted an all-water route to the spice lands. Spain was also eager to discover one. In 1494, to prevent conflict between these countries, the Pope* divided the world into two parts. Spain was allowed to trade and travel in one part, and Portugal in the other. At first, however, the boundary (Line of Demarcation) between the two parts of the world was not clearly drawn in the Eastern Hemisphere, where Southeast Asia is located. Thus Spain and Portugal were still not sure which lands they could claim there.

Early in the sixteenth century, a navigator named Ferdinand Magellan convinced the King of Spain that the Moluccas,* from which most of the spices came, were in Spain's part of the world. Magellan thought that he could reach these islands by sailing west, around the continent of South America. In 1519 he set out to find a westward sea route for Spain. On his voyage, Magellan came to the Philippines. He and his crew were the first Europeans to visit these islands. Magellan was killed in the Philippines, but one of his captains sailed on and returned to Spain. This was the first time a ship had sailed around the world.

Magellan's expedition succeeded in finding a westward water route to the spice lands, but this did not hurt Portugal's trade. Spain's westward route was very long and difficult, and the few Spanish ships that succeeded in reaching the Orient were captured by the Portuguese. Finally, in 1530, the Spanish and Portuguese signed a treaty, agreeing that the Moluccas were in Portugal's part of the world.

The Philippine Islands were also in Portugal's part of the world. However, in 1565, an expedition led by a Spaniard named Legaspi succeeded in establishing a colony there. Before the end of the sixteenth century, much of the Philippines was under Spanish control.

Portugal loses its power in Southeast Asia. Spain did not hurt Portugal's trade with the spice lands, but other European nations did. At the end of the sixteenth century, Dutch ships began coming to Southeast Asia. Portugal could not keep them out. One reason was that, because of low pay, many officials and soldiers sent by Portugal to Southeast Asia were more interested in gaining personal wealth than in working for their country. Another reason was that the Portuguese had made so many enemies in Southeast Asia that people there welcomed other traders. Before long, British, French, Swedish, and Danish trading ships were also coming to Southeast Asia.

Foreigners gain control of all of Southeast Asia except Thailand. The European traders who came to Southeast Asia did not want anyone to interfere with their trade. Warships and soldiers from Europe were sent to this region. Frequently, the Europeans attacked each

*See Glossary

Ferdinand Magellan reached the Philippine Islands on March 16, 1521. What route did Magellan follow to the Philippines? Why did he make this journey? What happened to him in the Philippines?

A Spanish fort in the Philippines. Over the years, all parts of Southeast Asia except Thailand were taken over by foreigners. Do research in this book and other sources to discover ways in which this was done.

other's ships and tried to destroy each other's trading stations and forts. Sometimes they used force to make people in Southeast Asia trade with them. The Europeans also helped to put down many wars between the nations of Southeast Asia so that trade could be carried on in peace.

The more powerful European countries gained control of large territories in Southeast Asia. What is now the country of Indonesia became a Dutch colony. Britain gained control of Burma and Malaya. The territory now occupied by North and South Vietnam, Laos, and Cambodia was taken over by the French. Spain controlled the Philippine Islands

until 1898, when they were taken over by the United States. Only Thailand remained independent.

Westerners* bring changes to Southeast Asia. At first, most of the Westerners who came to Southeast Asia wanted to obtain spices. Soon, however, it was discovered that this region could provide other valuable goods. There were rich mineral deposits, and the climate was good for growing tropical plants such as sugarcane and rubber trees. Mines and plantations were established, and roads and railroads were built to carry products to port cities where they could be shipped to markets overseas.

The Westerners who came to Southeast Asia helped the people here in many important ways. They brought peace to regions that had been torn by warfare. In several areas, missionaries introduced Christianity. Some hospitals and schools were started. New food crops such as potatoes and corn were brought in, and new methods of controlling irrigation and draining swamps were introduced. With peace, better health care, and increased food supplies, the population of Southeast Asia began to grow very rapidly.

The Western nations that gained control of Southeast Asia are remembered more by the people here for the ways they neglected this region. Most of the Westerners who came were mainly interested in making money. They thought of Southeast Asia as a source of raw materials for their own use. Since the Western nations wished to sell their own industrial goods in exchange for Southeast Asia's exports, little modern manufacturing was established in this region. In addition, people from the Western nations held nearly all of the important jobs. For this reason, only a few of Southeast Asia's people were able to get the kind of experience they needed for self-government.

The countries of Southeast Asia struggle for independence. Many Southeast Asian people were dissatisfied under Western rule and wished to be free again. Late in the nineteenth century, people in several Southeast Asian countries began to work for independence. The leaders of the independence movements were often Southeast Asian people who had learned about democracy and other political ideas while they were studying in Western schools.

As time went on, the leaders working for independence became increasingly impatient. In 1934, the United States made definite plans to grant the Philippines independence. However, the European nations that controlled other parts of Southeast Asia did not make any promises of complete freedom to their possessions. By the time World War II* began and the Japanese invaded Southeast Asia, many people here were ready to welcome anyone they thought might help them to achieve independence.

War ruins in Manila. After World War II began in Europe, the Japanese invaded Southeast Asia. Why was Japan eager to control this region? How did Japan win the support of people in Southeast Asia? Do you think the war helped speed independence for countries in this region? Why do you think as you do?

5 Independence and Government

The Japanese conquer almost all of Southeast Asia. A little past noon on December 8,* 1941, Japanese bombers with huge red suns painted on their wings roared toward Clark Field, outside the city of Manila. Minutes later, the air base was rocked by the sound of exploding bombs. When the attack was over, fifteen American Flying Fortresses and many fighter planes had been destroyed.

The fliers who had been eating lunch at Clark Field stared unbelievingly at the wrecked planes. They knew that the Japanese had bombed the American naval base at Pearl Harbor in Hawaii several hours earlier, but they had not expected the Philippines to be attacked so soon.

The attacks on Pearl Harbor and Clark Field were part of a Japanese plan to gain control of eastern Asia. The island country of Japan needed more petroleum, iron, and other raw materials than it was able to produce. It also needed markets for goods manufactured in its many factories. The Japanese decided that they would try to obtain the

*See Glossary

40

might have sent ships or planes to protect Southeast Asia. The United States declared war, but many of the American ships and planes in the Pacific area had been destroyed. Much time was needed to build more.

By August, 1942, almost all of Southeast Asia was controlled by Japan. The Japanese said that they wanted to drive the Westerners* out and restore Asia to the Asians. At first, this promise sounded good to the people who were striving for independence. The Japanese also impressed the people of Southeast Asia with their swift defeat of the Western forces in this region. Most of these once-powerful foreigners were imprisoned in Japanese concentration camps.

The Southeast Asians very soon realized that Japan's promise of "Asia for the Asians" was misleading. Japan only wanted to drive the Westerners out so that it could take over Southeast Asia. In many places, the Japanese treated the Southeast Asians more harshly than the Westerners ever had. A few Southeast Asian leaders worked with the Japanese. Some did so because they thought that by cooperating with the Japanese they might improve their country's chances for independence. However, in many parts of Southeast Asia, bands of guerrilla fighters were organized to oppose the invaders. The British and Americans furnished weapons to these bands whenever possible, even though some of them had Communist leaders. As the war continued, the Allies sent more and more men, ships, and planes to fight the Japanese. Finally, in 1945, Japan surrendered.

things they needed from other countries by force. As early as 1931 they invaded Manchuria, in northeastern China. Soon after World War II* started, the Japanese realized that this was a good opportunity to gain control of the rich natural resources of Southeast Asia. The Germans had overrun the Netherlands and France, and were threatening Britain. These three Allied nations could not send many soldiers to defend their colonies in Southeast Asia. First, the Japanese occupied the parts of Southeast Asia controlled by France. Then they bombed Pearl Harbor and other American military bases that

Most of Southeast Asia gains independence after World War II. The war increased the determination of Southeast Asia's people to gain independence. When the Japanese took over, they placed Southeast Asians in many important government positions, for there were too few Japanese officials to run the countries in this region. Near the end of the war, the Japanese tried to win support by granting some of the countries independence, though the Japanese actually remained in control. When the war was over, and the Japanese left, most Southeast Asians did not want the Westerners to return and try to establish their colonies again.

Within ten years after the end of the war, most countries in Southeast Asia had gained their independence. Some countries, such as Indonesia, had to fight bitterly before their independence was recognized. Others, such as the Philippines, were granted independence in an orderly manner.

The new nations of Southeast Asia face many problems. Southeast Asia's new nations had many problems to solve when they gained independence. Roads, railroads, and mines had been destroyed during the war. There were far too few industries and schools. Most of the countries did not have enough trained government leaders and skilled workers, and many of the people were poor, sick, and uneducated. It was hard for the newly independent countries to take care of their problems, for they had little experience in running their own affairs. In addition, they had little capital.*

Civil wars break out in several Southeast Asian countries. There is another reason why Southeast Asia's new governments have had difficulty in solving their problems. Many of the countries in this region did not exist until Westerners began gaining control over lands in Southeast Asia. Before that time, these countries were divided into many little independent territories. The Western nations simply

Education

See pages 137-140

Most countries in Southeast Asia are working hard to provide their people with an opportunity for more education. For example, the Philippine government considers schools so important that nearly one fourth of the money it spends each year goes for education. In 1940, fewer than three million Indonesian children attended school. Today, Indonesia has more than fourteen million children in school.

Much remains to be done, however. Many adults cannot read or write, and millions of children do not attend school. There are not nearly enough school buildings, well-trained teachers, and textbooks for the increasing number of people who want to study. In addition, the countries of Southeast Asia need to provide more opportunities for job training.

Organizations such as UNESCO and the governments of many outside countries are helping Southeast Asian nations solve their educational problems. For example, the United States has provided loans to pay for school construction. Technical advisors are teaching workers new farming methods and skills needed for jobs in modern industry.

You may wish to discuss the following questions with your classmates.
1. Do you think it is important for the countries of Southeast Asia to provide better educational opportunities? Why do you think this?
2. Do you think you would enjoy going to another country to try to help the people solve their educational problems? Explain your answer.

Training workers in Singapore. The countries of Southeast Asia need to provide more opportunities for job training.

LCOTRON AC GENERATOR
TYPICAL WIRING DIAGRAMS
GENERAL MOTORS
SERVICE

joined together territories they took over, established boundary lines, and set up colonial governments. Naturally, the different groups of people who were united under a colonial government usually felt no loyalty to it. Later, when the colony gained its freedom, some groups had no feeling of loyalty to the newly independent government, either. In some countries, such as Burma, different groups of people have rebelled and there has been civil war.

Southeast Asia is disrupted by a struggle for power between Communist and non-Communist forces. Communists have also caused serious problems for some of the new governments of Southeast Asia. In 1954, North Vietnam became an independent country with a Communist government. (See page 47.) A year later, South Vietnam also gained its independence. Soon South Vietnamese Communist guerrillas known as the Viet Cong began raiding villages, destroying railroads, and carrying on other acts of revolution against the government of South Vietnam. After 1960 they were supported by the government of North Vietnam,

Women army troops parading in Hanoi, North Vietnam. The North Vietnamese are aiding Communist guerrillas known as the Viet Cong in their war against the government of South Vietnam.

which hoped to bring South Vietnam under its control. The United States sent military advisors as well as money and equipment to South Vietnam to help the government remain in power.

By 1965, the guerrilla actions in South Vietnam had developed into a large-scale war. Regular North Vietnamese troops were fighting along with the Viet Cong against the South Vietnamese army. In January, 1965, American planes began bombing military targets in North Vietnam. By the end of the year, more than 180,000 American soldiers had

joined the South Vietnamese troops in their struggle against the Viet Cong and the North Vietnamese. Two years later, the number had risen to nearly 500,000. Smaller numbers of troops from Thailand, Australia, New Zealand, the Philippines, and South Korea also aided the South Vietnamese. Then on March 31, 1968, the United States halted its bombing in most of North Vietnam. Six weeks later, peace talks began in Paris, France. In 1969, the United States began a gradual withdrawal of its troops. However, a peace agreement has not yet been reached in Paris, and the war continues.

The war that began in South Vietnam has spread to neighboring countries. Communist troops from Vietnam have gained control of large areas in Laos and Cambodia. Government troops from South Vietnam, along with American troops, have attacked Communist supply routes and storage areas in these countries. Cambodia's army is also fighting Communist troops in the northern and eastern parts of that country.

In other parts of Southeast Asia, Communists have stirred up trouble in order to weaken the governments' authority. For example, they have encouraged strikes, and they have raided villages and plantations in order to frighten people into obeying Communist orders.

People in other parts of the world are helping Southeast Asia. Other countries are trying to help Southeast Asia's nations solve their problems. For example, the United States is providing money and sending teachers, farm experts, engineers, and other skilled people to countries in this region. Nations such as

Britain, Australia, France, the Soviet Union, and China are also sending this kind of aid. The United Nations is helping, too.

The countries of Southeast Asia will continue to need help for many years. Though progress is being made, they still need more roads, railroads, schools, and factories. Too few people have the opportunity to earn a good living, and there is still the danger of rebellion in some countries. Though outside help is needed in solving many of these problems, Southeast Asia's new nations do not want outsiders telling them what to do. These nations worked hard to gain independence, and now they are determined to guard it.

Government

The countries of Southeast Asia are governed in various ways. As the chart on the opposite page shows, the nations of Southeast Asia have several different kinds of government. For example, some are republics. Their governments are organized much like the government of the United States. Thailand and Laos are monarchies. In each of these countries, the head of state is a king. The monarch has little real power, however. One country in Southeast Asia, North Vietnam, is a Communist dictatorship.

Few of Southeast Asia's countries have truly democratic governments. Although most nations in Southeast Asia have a constitution based on democratic principles, few of them carry out these principles in the way the government of the United States does. The governments of

**Rules
and
Government**

See pages 137-140

The chart below shows that the countries of Southeast Asia are governed in several different ways. For example, Thailand and Laos are monarchies, although the monarchs hold little power. (The picture at left shows King Bhumibol of Thailand.) Several countries in Southeast Asia were established as republics. What is a republic? Does having this kind of government mean that a country is a democracy? Why? Why not? What likenesses and differences are there between governments in Southeast Asia and the government of our country?

FACTS ABOUT GOVERNMENT IN SOUTHEAST ASIA

BURMA

Burma became a republic in 1948. Its constitution provides for a two-house parliament. In 1962, however, General Ne Win took over the government, suspending the constitution and dissolving the parliament. He controls all executive, lawmaking, and judicial powers of the government.

CAMBODIA

Cambodia is a military dictatorship. Until 1970, the country was a kingdom headed by Prince Norodom Sihanouk. In March of that year, he was overthrown by military officers, and later Cambodia was declared a republic. In 1971, Premier Lon Nol abolished the constitution and took away the parliament's lawmaking powers. Lon Nol declared himself president in 1972.

INDONESIA

Indonesia is a republic with a one-house legislature. The members of another group, the Provisional People's Consultative Congress, are appointed and serve mainly as advisors. President Suharto, Indonesia's head of state, was elected by this group in 1968.

LAOS

Laos is a monarchy with a constitution based on democratic principles. King Savang Vatthana is the head of state, but Premier Souvanna Phouma, whom he appointed, does the real work of running the government. The parliament of Laos consists of an elected assembly and an appointed council.

MALAYSIA

Malaysia is a federation of thirteen states. Each of these states has its own head of state. In nine states, the rulers are similar to kings, inheriting their positions for life. These rulers elect one of their number to be the supreme head of Malaysia for five years. He appoints the heads of the other four states. Together, the thirteen heads of state form a council called the Conference of Rulers. Malaysia's laws are made by a two-house parliament.

THE PHILIPPINES

The Philippines is a republic. Its federal government is much like that of the United States, with an elected president, vice-president, and congress.

SINGAPORE

Singapore is a republic, with a one-house legislature elected by the people. The legislature elects the president, and the president appoints the prime minister, who actually runs the government.

THAILAND

Thailand is a monarchy, with King Bhumibol as the official head of state. However, the real power is held by a group of military officers, under the leadership of the prime minister. Late in 1971, the prime minister abolished the country's constitution and dissolved the lawmaking body.

NORTH VIETNAM

North Vietnam's constitution states that the government is a representative democracy. However, the Communist Party of North Vietnam actually controls the government. The lawmaking body meets only twice a year and simply gives formal approval to proposals made by executive bodies.

SOUTH VIETNAM

South Vietnam is a republic. President Nguyen Van Thieu was reelected for a second four-year term in 1971. However, since he was the only candidate, the people had no choice. Members of both houses of the legislature are elected.

some countries are headed by military leaders who allow little or no opposition to their rule. People who speak out against the government may be put in jail. Although elections are sometimes held, the people in power often find ways of preventing others from running against them.

Several facts help to explain why military leaders have come to power in Southeast Asia. In some countries, the people have been dissatisfied with the lack of progress being made in improving the standard* of living. (See page xvi.) Certain men have used this dissat-isfaction to help them seize power. Civil wars and a fear of communism have also helped military leaders gain control of some countries.

Several countries in Southeast Asia are making progress in developing stable democratic governments. Among these countries are the Philippines and Malaysia. The army officers who have controlled Indonesia's government since 1965 have made progress in solving many of the country's problems. In 1971, Indonesians elected members to the legislature. This was the first national election held since 1955.

The Parliament of Malaysia makes the country's laws. Malaysia is one of the countries in Southeast Asia that are making progress in developing stable democratic governments. What facts help to explain why many countries in this region have had difficulty in building stable governments?

Keep Up With Current Events

The countries of Southeast Asia are often in the news today. With your classmates, look for newspaper and magazine articles about events taking place in these countries. Look especially for articles about the problems the countries face and about steps being taken to solve these problems. Each person who brings in an article should read it to the class. Then the class as a whole should evaluate the significance of the event reported. You may wish to display the articles on a special bulletin board. Include pictures in your display wherever possible.

Be a Biographer

Two of the Southeast Asian leaders who worked for independence after World War II were Ho Chi Minh and Sukarno. Do research and write a short biography about one of these men. In your biography, include information about the following:

1. his early life
2. ways in which he influenced the independence movement
3. ways in which he affected government in his country after independence

Refer to pages 12-14 of the Skills Manual for help in locating information.

Thinking Together

As a class, discuss the following statement.
    A democratic government is only as good
    as the people make it.

Do you agree with this statement? Why? Why not? In your discussion, consider why many of the countries in Southeast Asia have failed to build stable democratic governments.

Investigate World War II in Asia

World War II involved nearly every part of the world. This war began in Europe in 1939. In December, 1941, the Japanese attacked Pearl Harbor in Hawaii and thus drew the United States into the conflict. With a group of your classmates, make a study of the war in Asia. First, do research to discover answers to the following questions.

1. Why did Japan begin building an empire in the late 1800's and early 1900's?
2. What type of government came to power in Japan in the 1930's?
3. What territories did the Japanese gain control of before their attack on Pearl Harbor? How did they gain control of these lands?
4. Why did the Japanese attack Pearl Harbor?
5. What were some of the most important events of the war in Asia after the United States entered the war? What other nations aided the United States?
6. What events led to Japan's surrender?

When you have completed your research, prepare a report based on your discoveries. Then present this report to the rest of your class. Your presentation will be more interesting if you illustrate it with pictures and maps. The suggestions on page 18 of the Skills Manual will help the members of your group work together successfully.

Use Your Imagination

Imagine that you served as a crew member on one of the ships Magellan commanded on his voyage from Spain in 1519. You were one of only eighteen crew members who eventually sailed all the way around the world. Tell the story of your voyage in words and pictures. In your story, include answers to the following questions.

1. What abilities and knowledge did Magellan have that enabled him to carry out this expedition?
2. How many ships were in Magellan's fleet?
3. What route did you follow?
4. What did you see during your voyage? What exciting things happened?
5. Were you ever dissatisfied or unhappy during the journey? If so, why?
6. What happened to the expedition after Magellan's death in the Philippines?

Feel free to use your imagination in writing your story, but be sure the information you present is based on facts. In addition to drawing pictures to illustrate your story, you may wish to make a map showing the route you followed around the world. Share your story with the rest of the class. The suggestions on page 17 of the Skills Manual will help you carry out this project successfully.

The floating markets on the canals of Bangkok provide one of the most colorful sights in Southeast Asia. Try to imagine what it would be like to visit the market shown in this picture. What do you think you would see? What sounds might you hear? What do you suppose you could discover about the people?

Part 3

People and Their Way of Life

Southeast Asia is a region of many different peoples and customs. Ways of life here differ greatly not only from one country to another but also within a single country. The text and pictures in Part 3 will help you discover what some of these differences are and why they exist. As you do research in the chapters in this section, you may also wish to consider the following questions.

- Do you think life in Southeast Asia would be similar in any ways to life in our country? Explain your answer.
- Which of the six largest cities in Southeast Asia would you most like to visit? Why?
- What are some of the ways in which people in Southeast Asia spend their leisure time?
- Do you think religion is important to the people of Southeast Asia? Why do you think this?

6 People

A visit to a farm village. We are walking along a narrow country road that leads to a small farming village in Thailand. The farm workers in the fields on either side of us have light-brown skin, straight black hair, and dark eyes that appear to be somewhat slanted. Most of these workers are not very tall. Some of the men are wearing cotton trousers and shirts much like those worn in the United States. Others have strips of cotton cloth tied around their waists and arranged to look somewhat like shorts. The women are dressed in loose-fitting blouses and long, bright-colored skirts. Many of the people are wearing large straw hats.

We are entering the village now. It is built along one bank of a river. The village houses are made of wood and bamboo, and have steep, pointed roofs that are thatched with nipa palm leaves. Each house is surrounded by a bamboo fence. Inside the fences are flowers, fruit trees, coconut palms, and small vegetable gardens.

One of the village women invites us into her home. We have to climb a flight of stairs to enter the house, for it is built on high posts. This protects the floor from floodwater when the river overflows its banks during the rainy season. When we glance at the open space under the house, we see that it

is used as a storage place for farm tools. A water buffalo, which the family uses for plowing, is kept there also.

We have reached the shady porch of the house now. The members of the family spend much of their time here. In the sleeping rooms that open off the porch we see wooden storage chests, and mats rolled up against the wall. These are unrolled at night and used as beds. There are no water faucets or electric lights in this house, although some bigger and newer houses may have them. The members of the family bathe every day in the river. They light their home with kerosene or coconut-oil lamps.

Our hostess is preparing dinner and invites us to stay. Her stove is made of clay, and looks somewhat like a flowerpot. When it is time to eat, we sit on the floor along with the family. We use a spoon made of coconut shell to dip rice, vegetables, and fish curry from the serving dishes into our bowls. Then we eat the food with our fingers.

The members of the family we are visiting are very pleasant and friendly to each other and to us. No one seems in a hurry to finish the meal and rush off to other activities. We can tell that the parents and children are very fond of each other and enjoy having visitors.

Most Southeast Asian people live in farming villages. Most of the people in Southeast Asia live in villages. The clothing these villagers wear and the customs they follow differ greatly from place to place. However, throughout Southeast Asia, most village people make their living as farmers. Many of

Meeting
Needs

See pages 141-142

A farm family. Most of the people in Southeast Asia live in villages. This chapter describes a visit to a farm village in Thailand. As you do research about the people of this village and their way of life, you may wish to discuss the following questions with your classmates.

1. How do the people of this village meet their needs for food, clothing, and shelter? In what ways do they use natural resources to help them meet these needs? What likenesses and differences are there between the ways they meet their physical needs and the ways you meet these same needs?

2. How do you suppose the villagers meet their various social needs? What goals might they have? Why do you think this?

3. In what ways might the people of this village meet their need for faith? Give reasons for your answer.

the farming villages are located on river plains and coastal lowlands. Some fertile highlands are densely populated, also. (Compare map on pages 8 and 9 with the map on page 57.)

Altogether, there are about 290 million people in Southeast Asia. This is about 85 million more than live in the United States. The number of people in Southeast Asia is becoming larger every year. More modern medical care, better food, and cleaner living habits have helped to bring this about. Fewer babies now become sick and die, and adults live longer than they used to. In parts of Java and Thailand, and on the Red River Delta of North Vietnam, there are more than 1,500 people living on each square mile of land.

Some Southeast Asian people live in large cities. In the densely populated parts of Southeast Asia there are some large cities. Here we may see wide, paved streets, automobiles, and modern office buildings. City people often wear clothing like ours. Some of them have electric lights, radios, piped water and gas, and other modern conveniences in their homes. Toward the outskirts of the city, however, are crowded neighborhoods of little houses much like the one we visited in the farm village.

Scattered groups of tribesmen live in the wilderness areas of Southeast Asia. After we leave the crowded cities and farmlands of Southeast Asia, we may travel for miles without seeing a single house or person. Large parts of this region are covered with swamps, and forested plains and mountains. In the remote highland areas are tribes of people who often live in a very primitive manner. Some are small, dark-skinned people who make their living as hunters and food-gatherers. Others have light-brown skin like the people of the lowlands. They usually clear small patches in the forest for farming.

HEALTH

The Westerners who established colonies in Southeast Asia built some hospitals and improved health conditions. However, disease is still a serious problem. Among the widespread illnesses in this region are malaria, dysentery, tuberculosis, and yaws. In some areas, health conditions are so poor that about half the babies die before they reach school age.

One reason why there is so much sickness in Southeast Asia is that many of the people have poor health habits. They drink impure water from ponds and canals, and do not practice proper sanitation. Many of them do not know that flies and mosquitoes carry disease. Often they cannot obtain the variety of foods needed for good health. Their main food is rice, which they prefer to eat after the brown, vitamin-filled outer covering has been removed.

There are not nearly enough fully trained doctors in Southeast Asia, but there are many medical workers with less training who treat common diseases successfully. There are also herb doctors and people who use magic ceremonies to try to restore health.

The governments of Southeast Asia's countries are trying to improve health conditions for their people. Organizations and governments in other parts of the world are also helping.
1. Do you think it is important for the people of this region to improve health conditions? Why do you think this?
2. How could cooperation between people in Southeast Asia and people in other parts of the world help solve the region's health problems?
3. Could education help people in Southeast Asia improve their health habits? Explain your answer.

The picture at right shows villagers listening to a lecture about malaria.

A tribal family in Thailand. Some of the tribesmen who live in Southeast Asia's remote highlands make their living as hunters and food-gatherers. Others clear patches of land in the forests for farming.

Many different groups of people live in Southeast Asia. If we visited the village of some mountain tribesmen in Thailand, we might find that the people there spoke a different language from that of the lowland villagers. Most lowland people in Thailand belong to a group called the Thai. However, the tribesmen in the highlands are divided into different groups that do not dress alike or speak the same language. All the countries of Southeast Asia have many different groups of people living within their borders. In Indonesia alone,

about twenty-five languages and more than two hundred dialects are spoken.

Some groups of people in Southeast Asia are newcomers from other countries. In years past, many people from China came to this region to work in oil fields and mines or on plantations. Today there are about 15 million Chinese in Southeast Asia. They run many of the shops and businesses. Most Chinese have kept their own language and customs instead of learning to live as the people of their new homeland do. They are not always welcomed by the

other people of Southeast Asia. In addition to the Chinese, there are people from India and Pakistan. There are also some Westerners.

Southeast Asia has borrowed religious ideas and customs from other lands. We find many different religions among the people of Southeast Asia. When we travel to the island of Bali, in Indonesia, we see temples where gods of the Hindu religion are worshiped. This religion developed in India many centuries before the birth of Christ. Traders from India helped to bring it to Southeast Asia. (See Chapter 3.) For a while Hinduism was very important throughout most of Southeast Asia, but as time went on other religions took its place. Today, the Hindu religion is important only on Bali and the neighboring island of Lombok. However, people in other parts of Southeast Asia still enjoy watching skilled dancers act out Hindu legends. (See picture on page 69.)

The religion that most people in Indonesia now follow is Islam. It was

The map at the right shows the density of population in different parts of Southeast Asia. Notice that many people live in some parts of Southeast Asia, and that other parts of this region are very thinly populated. Why do you suppose this is true? Are some areas better suited to meeting human needs than other areas? When you compare this map with the map on pages 8 and 9, you will see that most of the densely populated areas are lowlands. The map on page 85 shows that the crowded parts of Southeast Asia are generally the most important farming areas also.

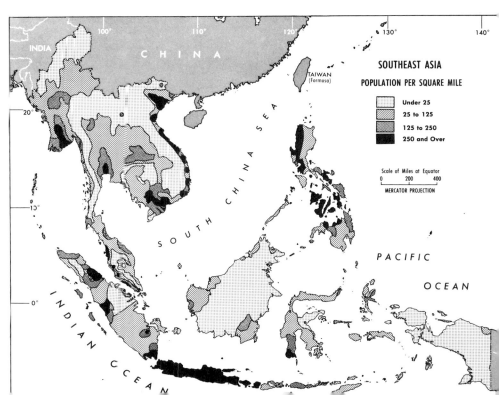

SOUTHEAST ASIA
POPULATION PER SQUARE MILE

Under 25
25 to 125
125 to 250
250 and Over

Scale of Miles at Equator
0   200   400
MERCATOR PROJECTION

founded in Arabia by a prophet named Mohammed, and was brought to Southeast Asia by traders and missionaries. Many people in Malaya also believe in Islam. Moslems* in Malaya and Indonesia have constructed beautiful buildings of worship called mosques. (See picture on page 33.)

In Thailand we see many tall, pointed pagodas, and temples with colorful roofs which turn up sharply at the corners. These have been built by the followers of a religious leader called Gautama Buddha, who lived in India about 2,500 years ago. Traders and missionaries from India, and later from Ceylon, helped to spread Buddhism to Southeast Asia. Today it is the main religion of Thailand, Burma, Cambodia, and Laos. Most Buddhist males in these countries become monks for some period of time during their lives. They shave their heads and dress in yellow or orange robes. Each morning they walk through the streets carrying bowls, which people fill with food.

Many Vietnamese people are Buddhists, also. They belong to a different branch of the religion from the one followed by their Southeast Asian neighbors, however. The Vietnamese learned about Buddhism mainly from Chinese monks, instead of from the Indians and Ceylonese who helped bring this religion to other parts of Southeast Asia.

*See Glossary

Offering food to a Buddhist monk in Thailand. Most Buddhist males in Thailand, Burma, Cambodia, and Laos become monks for some period of time in their lives. Each morning these monks walk through the streets carrying bowls for people to fill with food. Why do you suppose the monks get food in this way? Do research in other sources to find facts that support or disprove your answer.

The Vietnamese borrowed other ideas from China besides Buddhism. Many eat with chopsticks as the Chinese do, and follow the teachings of the Chinese philosopher Confucius, who lived about 500 B.C. Also, they worship the spirits of their ancestors.

Christianity is another important religion in Southeast Asia. Both Protestant and Catholic missionaries have come to this region. In most countries of Southeast Asia, only a small part of the people have accepted Christianity. In the Philippines, however, about nine tenths of the people are Christians. Most of them belong to the Roman Catholic Church.

Many Southeast Asian people whose religions came originally from other countries also practice spirit worship, or animism, just as their ancestors did long ago. The spirits are supposed to live in mountains, forests, streams, and other places. Some of the interesting customs we find in Southeast Asia have come from this belief in spirits. Almost every home in Thailand has a little spirit house in the yard or in the nearby area. The guardian spirit of the home is supposed to live here. Each day an offering of flowers, candles, and incense is placed in the house for the spirit. Shrines are also built for the worship of spirits.

Roman Catholic nuns in the Philippines. About nine tenths of the people in the Philippines are Christians. What facts about the history of the Philippines help to explain why Christianity is the country's chief religion? To answer this question, you will need to do research in other sources.

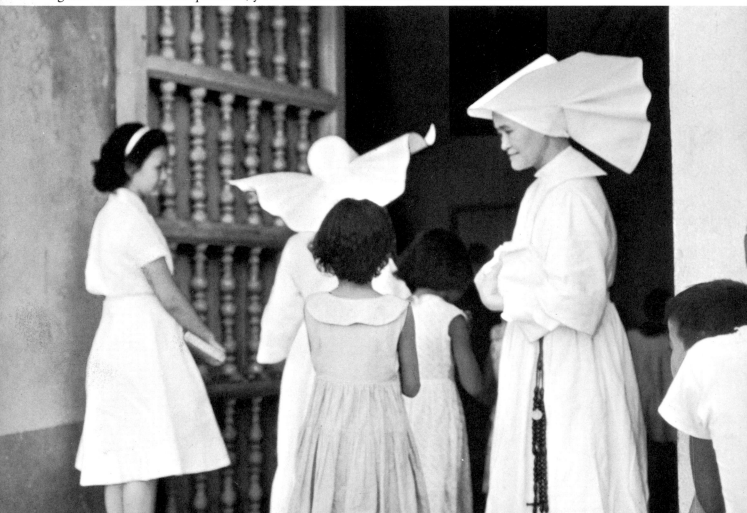

7 Cities

Southeast Asia's cities are interesting places to visit. Various groups of people, such as Chinese, Indians, and Malays, usually live in separate sections of a city. Some of the people dress in Western-style clothing, and some wear colorful native garments. Modern streets and buildings, as well as beautiful old temples and crowded neighborhoods of little thatch-roofed houses, can be seen in Southeast Asia's cities.

Although most people in Southeast Asia still live in villages, the cities in this region have been growing rapidly since World War II. Today, nearly sixty cities have populations of 100,000 or more. As the map on page 65 shows, some countries in Southeast Asia have more cities than others. Indonesia has a larger number of cities than any other country in this region.

The largest cities in Southeast Asia are Djakarta, Bangkok, Singapore, Saigon-Cholon, Rangoon, and Manila. All of them are seaports or river ports to which the products of nearby mines, forests, and farmlands are brought for export. Most of these cities are also national capitals. Let us learn more about the six largest cities in Southeast Asia.

Shoppers in Saigon. Many cities in Southeast Asia are very crowded. The populations of cities in this region have been growing rapidly in recent years. Why do you suppose this is so?

Djakarta is the capital of Indonesia and Southeast Asia's largest city. It has a population of nearly five million. Some of Djakarta's streets are very wide, but others are narrow and twisting.

Djakarta (population 4,774,000). The largest city in Southeast Asia is Djakarta, the capital of Indonesia. It is located in western Java, at the mouth of the Tjiliwong River. Since World War II, the population of Djakarta has grown rapidly, and the city is very crowded.

Djakarta is an important manufacturing and trading city. Among the many industrial plants here are iron foundries, sawmills, textile mills, and tanneries. Oil companies, shipping firms, and many other businesses have their offices in the city.

Some of Djakarta's streets are very wide, and others are narrow and twisting. Along many tree-shaded streets are attractive houses built by the Dutch when they ruled Indonesia. Most of these have now been taken over by the Indonesians. There are also many kampongs, or neighborhoods of native houses made of bamboo matting and thatch. Some of the interesting places to visit

There are hundreds of beautiful religious buildings in Bangkok. One of the most interesting is the Temple of the Emerald Buddha, which is located inside the walls that surround the Royal Palace. This temple contains a statue of Buddha about two feet high, carved from a single green stone.

Bangkok has wide, tree-lined boulevards and narrow alleys. The busiest street is called New Road. Along this street are government buildings, hotels, and banks, as well as little shops where goods such as jade are sold.

Singapore (population 2,033,000). Singapore is the leading port city in all of Southeast Asia. It is located on the southern shore of Singapore Island. (See map on page 136.) Much of the land on which the city stands was once a swamp. Hills were cut down, and the dirt was used to fill in the swampy areas. Along the harbor are three miles of wharves. In and near Singapore are tanneries, food-processing plants, sawmills, a tin smelter, and oil refineries. Other industries here include the manufacture of textiles, rubber goods, and cement.

Singapore is very crowded. Many people live in little huts, but there are also beautiful new apartment buildings and blocks of comfortable new houses. In the business section are large office buildings and banks. Several places in Singapore are named after Sir Stamford Raffles, who founded the city. Some of the interesting places to visit in the city are the Botanical Gardens and the three big Chinese amusement parks called the Great World, the New World, and the Happy World.

Saigon-Cholon (combined population 2,000,000). Saigon, South Vietnam's

in Djakarta are the museums, the botanical gardens, and the colorful markets.

Bangkok (population 2,300,000). Bangkok is the capital and the main port and manufacturing city of Thailand. It is located along the banks of the Chao Phraya River twenty miles from the Gulf of Siam. Canals called klongs branch off the river and cut through the city. On some of these waterways are floating markets where housewives may buy fish, vegetables, and other goods.

Singapore is located on the southern shore of Singapore Island. It is the leading port city in Southeast Asia. Why do you think Singapore has become such a great city? You may wish to do research in other sources to find facts that support or disprove your conclusions.

capital and largest city, is located on the Saigon River. Its largest suburb is the city of Cholon, which was founded in 1778 by a group of Chinese immigrants. Most of the factories in South Vietnam are in the Saigon-Cholon area. Although Saigon is about fifty miles from the sea, it is South Vietnam's leading port. Oceangoing ships sail on the Saigon River to and from this city.

Saigon is a very beautiful city, even though some areas have been damaged during the Vietnam War. Among the places of interest here are the stately presidential palace, the beautiful gardens of Tao-Dan Park, and the elaborate pagodas built in honor of Vietnamese heroes.

Saigon's neighbor Cholon has many canals that cut through the city. Many of the people here live in thatch-roofed houses built on stilts. Cholon is a leading rice-milling and rice-trading city.

Rangoon (population 1,759,000). Rangoon is the capital of Burma. As the map on pages 8-9 shows, it is located on the Rangoon River, about twenty miles from the sea. A canal links Rangoon with the Irrawaddy River, Burma's most important waterway. This canal has helped Rangoon become the country's leading port.

Rangoon is famous for its many pagodas. Towering over the other buildings in the city is one of the world's largest Buddhist temples, the Shwe Dagon Pagoda, which is covered with gold. (See the picture on pages 66 and 67.) Rangoon also has several fine parks and two beautiful lakes.

Manila (population 1,550,000). Manila is the main port of the Philippines. It is located on the island of Luzon, facing Manila Bay. (See the map on page 133.) Most of the Philippines' industry is located in the Manila area. There are machine shops, sugar refineries, cotton mills, and many other kinds of factories in and near the city.

The Pasig River divides Manila into two parts. On the south bank is the Intramuros, the old walled city that was built by the Spanish more than two hundred years ago. North of the Pasig is the newer section of the city. During World War II, nearly all of the Intramuros and much of the newer section were destroyed. Most of Manila has now been rebuilt. There are many modern buildings and wide avenues in the city. There are also little nipa palm huts much like those in Filipino* farming villages.

You can visit many churches in Manila. One of the most interesting is St. Augustine, the oldest stone church in the Philippines. It was the only church left standing in the Intramuros after World War II.

*See Glossary

Cities of Southeast Asia. Select a city in Southeast Asia you think you would like to visit, and do research about it in other sources. Then share your discoveries with your classmates.

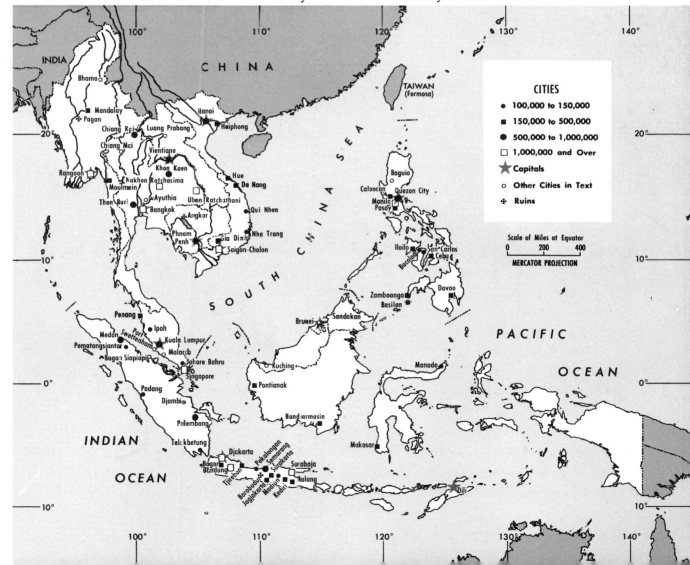

8 Arts

A visit to the Temple of Borobudur.
In a forest clearing on the island of
Java stands one of the world's most
magnificent religious structures—the
Buddhist Temple of Borobudur. This
vast stone temple is larger than the
great cathedrals of Europe. It was built
more than a thousand years ago, when
Buddhism was an important religion in
Indonesia.

As we approach Borobudur, we see
that it is a huge, stairlike pyramid. The
lower levels of this pyramid are square
in shape, and the upper three levels are
circular. Stairs lead from one level to
another. Crowning the whole structure
is a large, bell-shaped tower.

To examine the beauty of Borobudur
more closely, we climb slowly from
one level to the next. Delicate carvings showing scenes from the life of
Buddha decorate the walls of the lower
levels. On the circular upper levels are
seventy-two bell-shaped towers. We
glance through the small openings in
the wall of one of these towers and see
a statue of Buddha inside. We do not
know the name of the artist who carved
this image. Until recently, sculptors and
painters in Southeast Asia did not sign
their names to the pictures and statues
they created.

Religious architecture and art. We may
visit many beautiful religious structures besides Borobudur while we are
in Southeast Asia. Most of the oldest
and finest art and architecture in this
region was created to be used in worship. Southeast Asia's religious architecture differs from place to place. In

the countries of the Indo-Chinese Peninsula, where Buddhism is the main religion, there are many Buddhist temples
and pagodas. The vast, golden Shwe
Dagon Pagoda in Rangoon is one of the

The Need
for Faith

See pages 141-142

The Shwe Dagon Pagoda in Rangoon, Burma, is one of the world's largest Buddhist temples. Most of the finest works of architecture in Southeast Asia are religious structures. Why do you suppose this is so? Why might people spend much time and energy in creating such structures? Do you think it is important for people to have a beautiful building in which to worship? Why? Why not?

A statue of Buddha at the Temple of Borobudur. Many temples and churches in Southeast Asia are decorated with beautiful paintings and statues. However, mosques do not contain pictures or sculptures of people or animals. Why is this so? How are these places of worship decorated?

largest Buddhist temples in the world. People who visit it may buy small packages of gold leaf to place on its glistening surface. In the Philippines, where most of the people are Roman Catholic, there are great stone churches. Beautiful mosques have been built in the countries of Indonesia and Malaysia, where the religion of Islam is important. On the island of Bali are Hindu temples.

Carvings and paintings add to the beauty of Southeast Asia's fine religious buildings. In Buddhist temples we see beautiful murals and many different statues of Buddha. We also find exam-

ples of fine sculpture in Roman Catholic churches and Hindu temples. There are no pictures or statues of people or animals in mosques, however, for the religion of Islam forbids such images. Instead, the Moslems used carved designs and colored patterns for decoration.

Other traditional art and architecture. Through the centuries, artists and architects in Southeast Asia have also created works of art which have little to do with religion. Several beautiful pavilions have been built on the grounds of the royal palaces in this region.

Among the most interesting examples of nonreligious art in Southeast Asia are the slender wooden statues carved on the island of Bali.

Dancing and plays. When we visit a palace on the island of Bali, we see another of Southeast Asia's art forms. In the courtyard, young girls are performing a dance called the *Legong*. They wear crowns of gilded leather covered with masses of delicate flowers. Around their necks are wide, golden collars. Gold thread decorates the sashes which are wrapped around their bodies. The girls make graceful gestures as they dance. They are acting out an episode from an ancient Hindu story-poem called the *Ramayana*. Each motion they make has a special meaning.

We may see many different kinds of dances while we are in Southeast Asia. In Cambodia there is a dance called the *Leng Trot*, which is sometimes performed when the monsoon rains are late, to encourage them. In the beautiful *Tari Piring* of Sumatra, the dancers hold plates with lighted candles in their hands. Originally, this dance was performed after the harvest to honor the rice goddess. Dances are also performed at weddings and other celebrations in Southeast Asia.

Some of the finest dancing in Southeast Asia may be seen in dramas. Dancers wearing richly decorated costumes use carefully learned steps and gestures to dramatize ancient legends. In addition to these serious dramas, there are

Language

See pages 137-140

Legong dancers on the island of Bali. Dancers in Southeast Asia are highly skilled artists. The dances they perform generally tell a story. How are the dancers able to communicate ideas without speaking? What are some forms of dancing in our country in which the dancers tell stories without the use of words?

funny plays. While we are in Burma, we watch a musical comedy in which dancing girls and clowns tell jokes and keep the audience roaring with laughter.

Another interesting form of drama in Southeast Asia is the shadow-puppet play. The large, flat puppets used in these performances are made of leather. They are cut out and painted by hand.

A shadow-puppet play is being given tonight to entertain the guests at a family celebration in Indonesia, and we are invited. The performance will last until dawn, but we may leave and stretch our legs whenever we feel like it. When we arrive, we see that a screen made of white cotton cloth has been set up outside. It is lighted from the front by a bright oil lamp. The men sit in front of the screen and the women and children look at it from behind. The man who will give the puppet show has taken his place in front of the screen now. In a high-pitched voice he begins to tell an ancient Hindu legend, skillfully moving the puppets as he talks. The women and children who watch the performance from behind the screen see it as a shadow play.

Music. Musicians accompany the puppet plays, dances, and dramas that we see in Southeast Asia. The instruments used by orchestras in this region are carefully made and often very beautiful. There are gongs, drums, and instruments that resemble xylophones. There are also flutelike wind instruments, and stringed instruments somewhat like violins. Much of the music

we hear in Southeast Asia sounds strange to our ears. However, some of the popular music on the radio sounds more familiar. It reminds us of Hawaiian or South American music. Usually, this is because of the Portuguese and Spanish influence on music in all these areas.

Literature. Much of the literature enjoyed by people in Southeast Asia is very old. Ancient Hindu stories are familiar to people in many parts of this region. Other early literature includes

love stories, tales of magic, and episodes from the life of Buddha. Poetry is also well loved in this region. Often, poems and stories in Southeast Asia are passed on by one person telling another, for until recently most people in this region could not read.

Modern writers in some countries of Southeast Asia are producing short stories and novels about the everyday lives and problems of their people. Sometimes these modern writings are printed in newspapers, for few people can afford to buy books.

Modern arts. We may also find examples of modern painting, sculpture, and architecture in Southeast Asia. Some of Southeast Asia's modern artists have closely copied the methods of Western* artists. Others, however, are borrowing from the rest of the world what they feel is useful, and combining this with their country's ancient traditions.

*See Glossary

Musicians in Thailand. Musicians usually accompany the dances, dramas, and puppet plays that are performed in Southeast Asia. The instruments they play are carefully made and often very beautiful.

9 Festivals and Recreation

A festival in South Vietnam. It is a few nights before Tet, the Vietnamese New Year festival. We are going shopping in Saigon. All the stores are open, and the streets are crowded with people. Glowing colored lanterns hang in the trees, and the streets are lined with brightly decorated stalls. We stop at some of the stalls to buy New Year's presents for our friends, and armloads of fresh flowers to decorate the house.

On New Year's Eve, the bustling streets grow silent as everyone hurries home. In the house we are visiting, the members of the family have gathered before an altar. They are paying tribute to the spirits of relatives who have died, and are inviting them to share in the celebration.

The next morning, everyone in the family dresses in his best clothes and goes to the temple for prayer. Friends and relatives visit one another, and the children offer good wishes for the coming year to their parents and grandparents. In return, the children receive red envelopes containing money. The Vietnamese New Year is the most important holiday in South Vietnam. The date of Tet, like the date of Easter,

differs a little from year to year. This celebration comes during late January or early February.

Other festivals in Southeast Asia. There are a great many holidays besides New Year's in Southeast Asia. Buddhism, Islam, Christianity, and Hinduism are important in different parts of this region, and each of these faiths has its own celebrations. Chinese festivals are observed by the Vietnamese and by the people who have come to Southeast Asia from China. Harvesttime, the beginning and end of the rainy season, and holidays such as national independence days are also times of celebration.

Celebrations are held in honor of special events in a person's life, as well.

Meeting Needs

See pages 141-142

A Problem To Solve

The people of Southeast Asia celebrate many different festivals and other special occasions. In Burma, for example, a special ceremony is held when a boy enters a Buddhist monastery (above). In Cambodia, the planting season begins with a festival called the Plowing of the Sacred Furrow (left). Why are there so many special celebrations in Southeast Asia? In forming your hypotheses, consider ways in which these celebrations help people meet their physical needs, their social needs, and their need for faith.

See Skills Manual, pages 2-4

For example, in Burma there are celebrations at the time a girl's ears are pierced for earrings and at the time a boy enters one of the Buddhist monasteries. In Indonesia, celebrations marking important events such as these are called *selamatan.* If we attended a wedding *selamatan,* we would walk through an archway of palm fronds to the house or a special tent where the celebration was being held. There would be many guests besides ourselves, for everyone in the community would be invited. After the ceremony there would be a tremendous banquet. During the evening we would be entertained with music and dances. There might even be a puppet show. (See page 70.)

Leisure-time activities. In addition to celebrating festivals, people in Southeast Asia have other ways of spending their free time. Many businesses close for two or three hours at lunchtime so that people may rest during the early afternoon, when it is very warm. From dusk until bedtime, families often sit together and talk, or visit with neighbors. Sometimes a bonfire is lighted, and the young people have a contest to see who can make up the best verses to a song. At other times, village musicians perform, or a troupe of entertainers gives a play or puppet show. Movies, radio broadcasts, and television programs are popular in the areas that have them.

Games and sports. Southeast Asian people also enjoy games. In Thailand and several other countries, a group of young men will often form a circle and

Loyalty

See pages 137-140

Students in Thailand playing volleyball. Volleyball and several other team sports are popular in Southeast Asia. Choose a team sport you enjoy playing or watching, and then discuss these questions with your classmates.

1. Do you think loyalty is an important quality for team members to have? Why? Why not? In what ways do team members show loyalty toward one another?

2. In what ways do spectators show they are loyal to a team? Do you think loyalty is a good quality for spectators to have? Explain your answer.

Playing a ball game in Burma. In this game, the players keep the ball in the air with their feet.

pass around a ball made of rattan or hard rubber, keeping it in the air with their feet. Kite flying and cockfighting are other favorite pastimes. Boxing is very popular in the Philippines and in Thailand. One kind of Thai boxing allows the boxer to use his feet as well as his hands. On the island of Madura, in Indonesia, bull racing is an exciting sport.

In some of Southeast Asia's large cities there are stadiums where crowds of spectators enjoy watching the same sports as those played in Europe or the United States. One of the most popular of these sports is soccer. Frequently, the best soccer teams of different Southeast Asian nations compete with each other. They also compete with teams from Europe and from Australia. Volleyball, badminton, tennis, basketball, and cricket are other sports played in Southeast Asia.

Southeast Asian teams take part in several international athletic competitions. Both Indonesian and Malaysian teams have won the badminton championship of the world. In addition, Southeast Asian athletes have participated in the Olympic Games.

Thinking Together

In recent years, many people in Southeast Asia have been moving from rural areas to the cities. How do you think the lives of these people change as a result of moving? What problems might the people have in their new homes? If you were a Southeast Asian villager, do you think you would want to move to a large city? Why? Why not? Discuss these questions as a class. Be prepared to support your opinions with facts. The suggestions on pages 17 and 18 of the Skills Manual will help you hold a successful discussion.

Explore Village Life

With a group of your classmates, make a study of village life in Southeast Asia. You may wish to base your study on the description of village life in Thailand provided in Chapter 6, or you may decide to explore village life in some other country in this region. Use the following questions to guide your research.

1. How do most of the villagers earn their living?
2. In what kinds of houses do they live?
3. What are the main foods that they eat? How do they obtain these foods?
4. What religion or religions do most of the people practice?
5. What leisure-time activities do the villagers enjoy?
6. What kinds of clothes do the people wear?

When you have completed your research, decide as a group how you will report your discoveries to the rest of the class. You may wish to present information in one of the following ways.

1. Present a play in which you act out a typical day in the life of a family in the village. Decide which members of your group will play the parts of different members in the family. In your play, show how each member of the family spends his day. You may wish to wear costumes to show how the people of the village dress.

2. Draw pictures or paint a mural showing scenes of daily life in the village. Be prepared to explain the scenes to your classmates and answer any questions they may ask.

This book provides much of the information you will need. The suggestions on pages 12-14 and 18 of the Skills Manual will help you locate information and work together successfully on the project.

Examine Your Attitudes

Consider carefully the following statement.
> Our lives will be richer and more interesting if we learn to appreciate the ideas and customs of people who differ from us.

Do you agree with this statement? Why? Why not? Discuss your opinions with your classmates. In the discussion, support your opinion with examples.

Make Discoveries About Religious Festivals

As a class, make a study of various festivals and ceremonies observed by people of the Buddhist, Hindu, and Islamic faiths. To carry out this project, you should divide the class into three groups. Each group should be responsible for doing research and preparing reports about the festivals and ceremonies of one of these three faiths. If possible, illustrate your reports with pictures or drawings. The following books provide information that will be helpful in carrying out this project.

Dobler, Lavinia. *Customs and Holidays Around the World*. New York: Fleet Press Corporation, 1962.

Gaer, Joseph. *Holidays Around the World*. Boston: Little, Brown and Company, 1953.

An Adventure in Appreciation

With a group of your classmates, find pictures that show Southeast Asian painting, sculpture, and architecture. Then exhibit the pictures, together with descriptive information about each example of art. Be prepared to answer questions your classmates may ask. Finally, discuss the following question as a class. How can the arts of a country or region help us understand its people and its history? Support your opinions with examples.

Part 4
Earning a Living

The picture at right, which was taken outside a rice mill in Thailand, will help you make discoveries about some of the ways in which people in Southeast Asia earn their living. Study this picture, and then discuss the following questions with your classmates.

- The workers shown in this picture are drying rice outside the mill. Where do you think this rice came from? How do you think it was brought to the mill?
- What kinds of work do you think are done inside the mill? What do you suppose will be done with the rice processed here?
- Look at the red truck in the left-hand part of the picture. What product do you think this truck contains? Where might this product have come from?

At the end of your discussion, make a list of ways in which you think people in Southeast Asia earn their living. Then do research in Part 4 to find out if your conclusions are correct. As you explore the chapters in this section, you may also wish to consider the following questions.

- How do the different ways of earning a living in Southeast Asia help people meet their needs?
- What facts help to explain why many people in this region do not earn a good living?

10   Farming

Southeast Asia is one of the world's important farming regions. In most parts the climate is always warm, so crops can be raised all year. Most of this region also has heavy rainfall. Some parts of Southeast Asia produce large quantities of rice, rubber, and other products to sell to foreign countries. There is enough unused land here to raise even larger amounts of farm products.

Less than one tenth of the land is used for farming. Only about nine out of every hundred acres of land in Southeast Asia are planted in crops. In most of Southeast Asia, the main farmlands are on river plains and coastal lowlands. The silt that the rivers wash down from the mountains helps to make these lowlands fertile. On the island of Java, people have made level fields on the slopes of volcanoes by building stairlike terraces. Ashes and other materials from the volcanoes help to make the soil in these fields very rich.

Plowing a rice field on Java. Most of the workers in Southeast Asia earn their living by farming.

Using Natural Resources

See pages 137-140

A tea plantation on Java. In colonial times, Westerners* established many plantations in Southeast Asia.

1. What facts about the natural resources of this region help to explain why Westerners started these large farms?

2. Do you think farmers in Southeast Asia today make as good use of the natural resources available to them as they might? Give reasons for your answer.

*See Glossary

Swampy lowlands and forested mountains cover much of the rest of Southeast Asia. The soil in many of these wilderness areas is poor, for heavy rains wash out the minerals and other materials needed by plants. Also, mosquitoes carrying malaria and other diseases make some of these areas unhealthy places in which to live. If the mosquitoes were controlled, swamps drained, and land cleared and fertilized, Southeast Asia could have more farmland.

Crowded farmlands of Southeast Asia. Some of the farmlands of Southeast Asia are very crowded. (Compare the map on page 85 with the one on page 57.) In the Red River Delta of North Vietnam and on the island of Java, tiny fields cover the countryside like pieces of a puzzle fitted closely together. Many farmers in these densely populated areas raise two crops on the same land each year. Even so, they often cannot produce all the food they need.

Less-crowded farmlands of Southeast Asia. Some lowlands in Southeast Asia have been cleared for farms only in the last one hundred years. Peasants using simple tools have drained huge swamps in the Irrawaddy Delta of Burma. Other farming areas have been opened up in Cambodia and Thailand. As yet, the newer farmlands of Southeast Asia are not as crowded as those

In northern Luzon (left), many farmers raise rice on mountain slopes. What facts help to explain why they do this? Comparing the map below with the map on page 133 will help you answer this question.

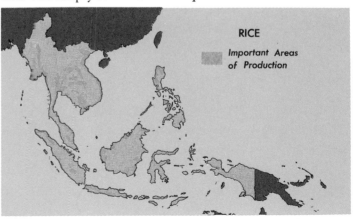

RICE

Important Areas of Production

An experimental farm in Burma. Few farmers in Southeast Asia have tractors or other modern farm equipment. Why do you think this is so? What are some of the problems faced by farmers in this region? What steps are being taken to help solve these problems?

settled earlier. The farms are larger, and farmers usually raise only one crop a year. Even so, they are generally able to produce more than they need. Large quantities of rice are exported from these newer farmlands.

Plantations in Southeast Asia. The map on page 85 shows that Southeast Asia also has plantations. These produce rubber, palm oil, tea, tobacco, copra, and other agricultural products for export. Most of Southeast Asia's plantations were established by Westerners, but many of them have come under local control.

Farms in forest clearings of Southeast Asia. Scattered throughout the remote forests of Southeast Asia are still other farmlands. Primitive tribesmen who live in these wilderness areas practice shifting cultivation. They cut down and burn trees to clear small patches of land for farming. Then they plant their crops among the burned stumps and fallen tree trunks. Every few years, when the soil has lost its fertility, the tribesmen move on and clear new land.

Problems that Southeast Asia's farmers face. About three fourths of Southeast Asia's workers make their living in agriculture. Most of these people use primitive farming methods. They plant and harvest their crops by hand and use simple tools such as hoes and sickles. Water buffalo or oxen pull their plows. Sometimes rats, grasshoppers, or other pests destroy part of the harvest. Most of Southeast Asia's farmers need to use more fertilizer. In the parts of this region that have a dry season, irrigation is needed to help crops grow when there is no rain. Also, better roads should be built so that farmers may transport their products to markets more easily.

There are other serious problems that farmers in parts of Southeast Asia face. In many countries of this region, only one third to one half of the farmers own their farms or are free from heavy debts. Landowners often charge high rents, and men who lend money to farmers or market their goods often demand unfair payment for these services. Some way must be found to help farmers obtain land of their own, or rent it at reasonable prices. They must also be given an opportunity to receive a fair share of the profits from their harvests.

Some work is being done to help Southeast Asia's farmers. In several countries, land* reform laws have been passed. Cooperatives are being started in some places to help farmers market their goods and borrow money. In addition, farm experts from other parts of the world are working with Southeast Asians to discover ways of raising better crops and livestock For example, new varieties of rice were developed in the Philippines. These new varieties help farmers raise two to three times as much rice as they could in the past.

Rice is Southeast Asia's most important crop. When we take a helicopter ride over the farmlands of Southeast Asia, we fly across many rice fields. In the lowlands we see farmers scattering rice seeds in little plots of ground called seed-beds, which will later be flooded. The young rice plants will grow here for about a month. Then they will be moved to larger flooded fields where they will grow and ripen. Flooded fields are also found on the terraced mountain slopes of Java and Luzon. (See picture on pages 82 and 83.) On hilly farms where the land has not been terraced, farmers often grow dry rice, which is raised in much the same way as wheat.

About five out of every ten acres of farmland in Southeast Asia are planted in rice. (See map on page 83.) It is the most important food crop of the people in this region. Rice is also an important export crop. Thailand and Burma raise more rice than they need, and these countries are among the world's main rice exporters. The rice is shipped to

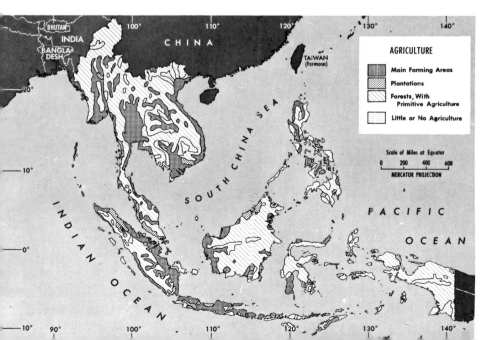

Use the map at left, the map on pages 8 and 9, and the text in this chapter to help you answer the following questions.

1. On what types of land are most of Southeast Asia's farms located?
2. What does the term "primitive agriculture" mean? Why do you think there is little farming other than primitive agriculture in West Irian?
3. On which of Indonesia's five main islands do you think farming is most important?

India, Japan, Indonesia, and other crowded countries that do not produce enough food for their people.

Other crops that Southeast Asians raise to use themselves. Southeast Asian farmers raise other food crops besides rice. Corn, sweet potatoes, and other crops that need less moisture than rice are grown in the drier parts of this region. Most farmers raise vegetables such as beans which provide some of the proteins that people in our country get from meat. Mango, papaya, and other fruit trees often grow around village houses. Sugarcane is also raised.

Farm products that Southeast Asia sells to other countries. Southeast Asia exports other farm products besides rice. When we drive down the western coast of the Malay Peninsula we pass many large rubber plantations. We notice that the tall rubber trees have been planted in perfectly straight rows. Early in the morning, we see workers carefully make slanting cuts in the bark of the trees to gather latex, the fluid from which rubber is obtained. The workers collect the latex in small bowls fastened to the trees, and then pour it into large pails. Later, it is weighed and carried in a tank truck to the plantation's central building. There, an acid is added to the latex to thicken it. Then it is pressed thin between rollers and cut into pieces about the size of bath towels.

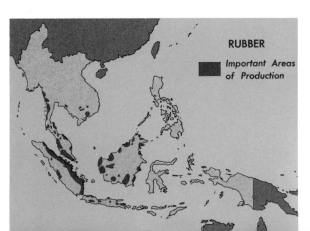

RUBBER

Important Areas of Production

Rubber is one of Southeast Asia's most important farm products. Why do you think this is so? Which countries lead the region in rubber production?

Early in the morning, a worker on a rubber plantation makes a slash in the bark of a rubber tree. Latex, the fluid from which rubber is made, is collected in the small bowl fastened to the tree. Do research to discover the remaining steps in rubber production.

These are dried for several days before being packed for export.

Southeast Asia provides more than four fifths of the world's natural rubber. Malaysia and Indonesia are the main producers. Much of the rubber in Southeast Asia comes from the trees that are grown on large plantations. Increasing amounts, however, are obtained from small patches of trees that are owned and cultivated by Southeast Asian or Chinese farmers.

When we travel along the coasts of Southeast Asia, we frequently pass groves of coconut trees. The dried meat of coconuts, called copra, provides vegetable oil for soap, margarine, and other products. Three fourths of the world's copra comes from Southeast Asia. Oil

Floating coconuts to market. Southeast Asia is the world's largest producer of coconuts. What is the dried meat of coconuts called? What are some of the products made from this raw material?

A worker in the Philippines strips fibers from abaca plants. What is the main use for these fibers? Why has the market for abaca declined in recent years? What other crops of Southeast Asia are in less demand now?

palms grown in this region also provide large quantities of vegetable oil.

Other tropical crops are grown in Southeast Asia. Coffee, tea, and spices are important exports. Indonesia raises larger quantities of these crops than any other country in this region. Cinchona trees are also grown in Indonesia. A medicine called quinine is obtained from the bark of these trees. Silky kapok, used in making life belts and pillows, is another export crop that comes from trees in Southeast Asia. In the Philippines are many fields of abaca. The long, coarse fibers obtained from this plant are used to make strong rope that does not wear out quickly in salt water. Pineapples, bananas, and tobacco are also exported from the tropical farmlands of Southeast Asia.

Synthetic products are replacing Southeast Asia's farm exports. The nations of Southeast Asia depend almost entirely on the export of raw materials such as rubber, copra, and abaca in order to earn the money they need. However, many of these raw materials are now being replaced with products developed by modern science. Nylon is making abaca unnecessary, and new drugs are being used instead of quinine. Many people are using detergents in place of soap, which is often made of vegetable oil obtained from copra. The production of synthetic rubber has increased rapidly in recent years. This may eventually ruin the market for Southeast Asia's natural rubber. The problem that synthetic goods present to countries in Southeast Asia remains to be solved.

11 Natural Resources

Southeast Asia is a treasure-house of natural resources. The countries of Southeast Asia have a wealth of natural resources. Many parts of this region have fertile soil and a climate that is well suited to farming. (See Chapter 10.) The mines, forests, and fisheries of Southeast Asia yield a wide variety of useful products.

In the past, several Western* nations wanted to make certain they could obtain raw materials from Southeast Asia. They gradually gained control of all of this region except Thailand. Westerners established mines and plantations here. Today, although nearly all of Southeast Asia is independent, people from other parts of the world still control many of the region's mines and plantations.

Southeast Asia sells large quantities of its raw materials to other parts of the world, for it does not have enough factories to use all these goods. In some years, other countries pay low prices for the raw materials that the region exports. Then, many people who have jobs in industries that produce or prepare goods for export earn less money than usual.

Most Southeast Asian countries are trying to establish more factories. This will help them make better use of their raw materials and also provide jobs for large numbers of people.

Mineral Resources

Southeast Asia is the world's leading source of tin. To learn about one of the most important products exported from Southeast Asia, let's travel to a tin mine outside of the city of Kuala Lumpur, in Malaya.* Here we see an enormous dredge floating on an artificial pond. Huge

*See Glossary

The port of Cebu, in the Philippines. Southeast Asia is rich in natural resources. However, few of these resources are used within this region. Instead, large quantities of products from Southeast Asian mines, forests, fisheries, and plantations are shipped to countries in other parts of the world. Why is this so?

Mining tin near Kuala Lumpur, in Malaya. This picture shows one of several methods of mining tin in Southeast Asia. Describe what is happening. What are three other ways in which tin is mined?

buckets at one end of the dredge are scooping up mud that contains tin ore. Inside the dredge, the mud is passed through machines that separate the tin ore from the waste materials. About one third of the tin produced in Malaya is mined with dredges like this. Most of them are owned by European companies.

The next day we learn about other methods of tin mining used in Malaya. At a tin mine operated by a Chinese company, we watch workers use powerful streams of water to wash dirt containing tin ore down from the sides of a huge pit. The mud is pumped into a long trough where the ore is separated from the waste materials. Later in the day, we see some women on the bank of a stream swirling muddy water around in large wooden bowls. This simple method separates pieces of tin ore in the water, which are heavy, from the sand and mud. We also visit one of the few dry tin mines in Malaya. Here huge power shovels dig into a hillside that is rich in tin ore. The manager of the mine tells us that, through the centuries, rivers have washed away large quantities of dirt containing tin ore from hills like this one. The giant dredge we saw at the beginning of our trip obtains its ore from dirt these rivers deposited in the lowlands.

Almost half of the world's tin comes from Southeast Asia. Much of it is mined in Malaya. However, Thailand, Indonesia, Burma, North Vietnam, and Laos also have tin mines. (See map below.) Some of the tin ore mined in Southeast Asia is taken to smelters in

The map at right shows the location of the main mineral resources in Southeast Asia. As you can see, this region is rich in mineral resources. Use this map, the map on pages 8 and 9, and the text in this chapter and Chapter 12 to help you discover answers to the following questions. (You may wish to do additional research in other sources.)

1. Which countries in Southeast Asia do not have any important deposits of petroleum? tin? iron ore? How do you think these countries could get supplies of these resources?

2. What relationships can you discover between mineral resources and crafts and industries in Southeast Asia?

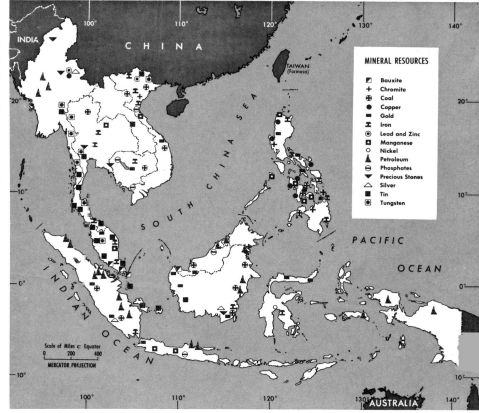

Workers drilling for petroleum in the Philippines. Countries in Southeast Asia have been trying to discover new oil fields. Why do you suppose this is so?

Malaya, Singapore, Thailand, or Bangka in Indonesia. There it is processed to make shiny bars of tin. These are sent to factories in other countries to be used in making cans and other tin products. Most of the remaining ore is shipped to smelters in Europe, the United States, or Japan.

Southeast Asia is the main petroleum-producing region of eastern Asia. Now let us visit an oil field on the island of Sumatra, in Indonesia. On the way we travel through steamy rainforests. Soon, we see ahead of us the tall derricks of an American oil company. When we tour the oil field, we find that nearly all of

learn that little oil is now produced in the rest of eastern Asia, we realize how important Southeast Asia's oil fields are. Each year, more and more people in Southeast Asia use oil products as cooking fuel and for other purposes. Tankers carry oil from this region to Japan, Australia, and other countries. In the large cities there are also many small electric plants in which the generators are run by diesel engines.

Southeast Asia produces bauxite and other valuable minerals. The map on page 93 shows us some of the other minerals produced in Southeast Asia. Bauxite is mined in Indonesia and Malaysia. This ore is the main source of aluminum, a lightweight metal that is used in making airplanes, pots and pans, and other goods. Iron ore is found in Malaysia, the Philippines, North Vietnam, and other parts of Southeast Asia. The Philippines is among the world's five leading producers of chromite, which contains chromium, a metal used in making steel and for plating automobile parts. Lead, manganese, phosphates, gold, and sapphires are among other minerals found in Southeast Asia. Almost all of the mineral products of this region are exported. Many are shipped to Japan and the United States.

Southeast Asia does not have enough high-grade coal. One resource that most of Southeast Asia lacks is good-quality coal. Without this fuel it is difficult to establish modern industry. North Vietnam is the only part of Southeast Asia that produces high-grade coal. Some of the low-grade coal mined in other parts of the region is used for fuel in steam locomotives. Electric power plants also use low-grade coal to heat water and

the highly skilled workers are Indonesians. An engineer tells us that there are Indonesian as well as foreign oil companies in Sumatra.

Indonesia, Burma, and the British protectorate of Brunei produce about 2 percent of the world's oil. This may not seem like very much. However, when we make steam. The steam runs generators that produce electricity. However, Southeast Asia needs much more electricity than these plants produce.

Waterpower

Waterpower is an important natural resource of Southeast Asia. Although Southeast Asia does not have enough good-quality coal, it does have vast supplies of waterpower. Many rivers flow through this rainy, mountainous region. If more dams and hydroelectric power plants were built on these rivers, the people could have all the electricity they need.

Almost every Southeast Asian country is trying to make greater use of its waterpower. A huge dam has been constructed on the Ping River in Thailand. South Vietnam, Laos, Cambodia, and Thailand are cooperating in a project sponsored by the United Nations to develop the waterpower of the mighty Mekong River. Several dams have been built or are now under construction.

A Problem To Solve
The picture at right shows the construction of a dam in Thailand. The people of Southeast Asia are building many dams and hydroelectric power plants. Why is this so? In forming hypotheses to solve this problem, consider how these projects will affect:

1. industry in Southeast Asia
2. farming in this region
3. the daily lives of the people in Southeast Asia

See Skills Manual, pages 2-4

Using
Natural
Resources

See pages 137-140

Djatiluhur Dam in western Java has greatly increased Djakarta's supply of electricity. Other recently completed projects include the Maria Cristina plant in the Philippines and the Cameron Highlands power project in Malaysia.

Rivers can also be used to furnish water for crops. Some of the dams that are being built in Southeast Asia will hold back water for irrigation during the dry season. This will help farmers raise much more food. The dams will also help protect the land from floods during the rainy season.

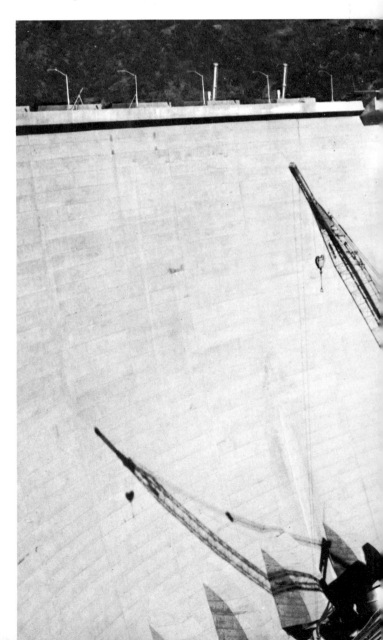

Forest Resources

Forests are another important natural resource of Southeast Asia. Forests cover about six tenths of the land in Southeast Asia. Like the waterpower in this region, the forests are not yet used as fully as they could be. One reason is that many different kinds of trees often grow in one area. It is difficult and expensive to reach the valuable trees and remove them from the forests. In places where there are no navigable rivers, lack of transportation is another problem. Mountains and marshes make it hard to build roads and railroads, which are needed to transport logs to where they can be used.

In spite of these problems, Southeast Asia's forests are important. They provide the people with wood for fuel, for building houses and furniture, and for many other useful things. Some forest products are sold to other countries.

The forests of Southeast Asia differ from place to place, for the amount of rainfall and the distance above sea level are not the same everywhere. Let's learn what these different forests are like.

The tropical rainforests. In parts of Southeast Asia where it rains all year round there are tropical rainforests. These are found in lowland areas, and on mountain slopes that are less than four thousand feet above sea level. The trees that grow in these areas are tall, and they remain green throughout the year. Their leafy branches form a roof through which the sun can scarcely shine. High in this green roof are climbing vines and wild orchids.

Many different kinds of trees grow in the tropical rainforests. Among these are the valuable Philippine mahogany trees. Wood from these trees is exported to Japan and other countries, where it is made into products such as furniture.

The monsoon forests. In Burma, Thailand, and other parts of Southeast Asia

Elephants moving teak logs in Thailand. Teak trees grow in the monsoon forests of Southeast Asia. Strong, long-lasting teakwood is excellent for building ships and for making furniture.

that have a dry season, there are monsoon forests. They are more open than rainforests, and some sunlight can shine down between the trees. Monsoon forests differ from rainforests in other ways as well. Most of the trees that grow in monsoon forests lose their leaves during the dry season. Also, certain kinds of valuable trees sometimes grow together in groups instead of being mixed in with other trees. As a result, workers can harvest timber more easily in monsoon forests than in rainforests.

On hillsides in the monsoon forests we may see large groups of teak trees. Sometimes they grow to be 150 feet high, with leaves that are two feet long. Their strong, long-lasting wood is good for building ships and making furniture. Elephants are often used to drag teak

What are the other three types of forests in Southeast Asia? Why do the forests differ from place to place? Why are Southeast Asia's forests important to the people of this region?

logs through the forests to streams. From there, the logs are floated to sawmills in Rangoon or other cities. Teak is one of the main forest products that Southeast Asia sells to other parts of the world.

Mountain forests. On mountain slopes above the rainforests and monsoon forests are oaks and other trees like those found in cooler climates. Pines sometimes grow on the higher slopes. Paper mills have been built in Indonesia to use the wood from the pine forests of northern Sumatra.

Coastal forests. Along the coasts of Southeast Asia are different kinds of forests. Mangrove forests grow on swampy beaches where the tide washes in and out. The strange-looking trees that grow here send down roots from their branches. Many Southeast Asian people obtain firewood from mangrove forests. They also make charcoal from the wood obtained here. Above the high-tide line grow many nipa palms. Their leaves are used to make baskets and thatched roofs. Along sandy, well-drained beaches there are many groves of swaying coconut palms. Coconut meat is dried and exported in large quantities from Southeast Asia.

Other forest products. The freighters that sail from Southeast Asia carry other forest products besides lumber and dried coconut meat. Vinelike climbing plants in the tropical rainforests provide a woody material called rattan, which is used in making baskets, furniture, and umbrella handles. Other forest products are gums and resins that are used in chewing gum, varnish, soap, and medicines. Wood to be used for making

incense, which gives off a pleasant smell when burned, is also gathered in the forests of Southeast Asia.

One of the most interesting and useful forest products of Southeast Asia is bamboo. This large, treelike plant belongs to the grass family. It often grows wild in places where forest fires have destroyed trees. Farmers also grow clumps of bamboo around their houses. The hollow stems of some kinds of bamboo grow to be eight inches across. Bamboo is an important building material in Southeast Asia.

Fishing

A visit to the Great Lake in Cambodia. It is a hot day early in the dry season, and we are going to take a helicopter

Trapping fish in the **Great Lake of Cambodia.** During the rainy season, many fish swim from the Mekong River into the flooded forests that border the Great Lake. When the rainy season ends and the water goes down, fishermen place traps to catch these fish as they swim out of the forests.

trip to the Great Lake in Cambodia. (See map on page 125.) This is the best inland fishing ground in Southeast Asia. At least 50,000 tons of fish are caught here each year.

Our trip begins on the coast, at one of the mouths of the great Mekong River. We follow the Mekong inland until we come to the Tonle Sap River. This waterway connects the Mekong to the lake. (See map on page 125.) As we fly northward along the Tonle Sap it enters a great area of mud flats. We fly across these until we come to the swamp forests that border the lake. At a small fishing village, we leave our helicopter and hire a boat.

One of the boatmen tells us that during the rainy season the lake is about four times as large as it is now and nearly ten times deeper. The Mekong River is so high then that some of its waters flow up the Tonle Sap River into the lake and flood the surrounding forests. Huge schools of young fish from the Mekong swim into the flooded forests at that time. Finding plenty of food there, these fish grow very quickly.

When the rainy season ends, the lake becomes smaller and shallower. As the water goes down, the fish that have been living in the flooded forests swim into deeper parts of the lake or start back toward the Mekong. Then the busiest time of the year for the lake fishermen begins.

We sail slowly around the lake to see different groups of fishermen at work. One group is collecting fish from giant traps. (See picture above.) The traps are placed in the water near the edge of the flooded forests to catch the fish as they swim out. Farther along we pass some men in little wooden boats, scooping up fish in dip nets. Out in the middle of the lake, several boatloads of men are working together to encircle a school of fish with a huge net.

Later in the day we visit a fishing village and learn how the fish are processed to keep them from spoiling. This must be done quickly, for there are no refrigerators. In one place we stop to watch some villagers mixing salt and small fish in wooden vats. The mixture will ferment and make a tasty, strong-smelling sauce that is eaten with rice and vegetables. In another part of the village, women and girls are cleaning and salting fish. Later, these fish will be spread out on huge racks to dry in the sun. Dried fish are exported from the Great Lake to other parts of Southeast Asia. In addition, bamboo cages filled with live fish are floated down rivers to cities along the coast. We do not see any canneries near the Great Lake. However, we learn that a few have been established in other parts of Southeast Asia.

Many people in Southeast Asia eat fish instead of meat. Throughout Southeast Asia, many people eat fish instead of meat. There are several reasons for this. Fish is plentiful, and meat is scarce and expensive. The climate here is too hot for some kinds of cattle. Also, religious beliefs discourage people from eating meat. Moslems believe that pork is unclean, while Buddhists think it is wrong to kill any animals, even for food.

Farm families catch many of the fish they eat. As we travel through Southeast Asia, we find that farm families catch many of the fish they eat. These part-time fishermen use hooks and lines, and several kinds of nets and homemade traps. They fish in ditches, rivers, ponds, and swamps. Along the marshy coasts of several islands in the Philippines and Indonesia, fish are raised in artificial saltwater ponds. Flooded rice fields are also stocked with fish.

Many fish are caught in shallow coastal waters. In addition to the inland fishing waters we have learned about, Southeast Asia has sea fisheries. Warm, shallow waters border many of the coasts in this region. These waters are rich in the foods needed by fish. Among the fish

caught here are mackerel, tuna, anchovies, and different kinds of shellfish. Most of the boats used by coastal fishermen are quite small and frail-looking. Many fishermen do not even use boats. Instead, they build fish traps near the shore or wade through shallow water, catching fish in nets.

One of Southeast Asia's important sea-fishing centers is the port of Bagan Siapiapi, in eastern Sumatra. The fish brought to this port are salted, dried, or smoked. Then they are shipped to many other parts of Southeast Asia.

What is being done to improve sea fishing in Southeast Asia. Several Southeast Asian countries are working to improve their sea fisheries. In Malaysia there is the Marine Fisheries School, where fishermen are taught how to use boats with motors. This school also teaches the fishermen skills that help them sail out to sea farther and more safely. Teams of Japanese fishermen have been invited to South Vietnam to teach the people there better fishing methods. Shipyards in Indonesia and other Southeast Asian countries are learning to build better fishing vessels. In these and other ways, the countries of Southeast Asia are trying to increase the supply of one of their most important foods—fish.

Fishing off the coast of Java. Throughout Southeast Asia, many people eat fish instead of meat. What facts help explain why this is so? What are some of the kinds of fish caught in this region?

12   Crafts and Industry

Handicrafts are important in Southeast Asia. Many of the household articles and tools used by villagers in Southeast Asia are made by hand. Let's visit a village house in Malaya* to watch a woman weave a mat out of pandan leaves. She cut these long leaves from trees growing around the family rice field. It took several days to prepare the leaves for weaving. They were cut into strips, soaked in water, dried, and then dyed. Now the woman skillfully weaves the different colored strips together to form a mat with a beautiful pattern. When we leave her house and walk through the village market, we see baskets, bags, and hats that were also woven by hand.

Several days later, when we are in Java, we watch a group of workers making delicate designs on cotton cloth. One woman is drawing the outline of a design on a piece of fabric. Later, another woman will put hot wax on all parts of the design except those that are to be dyed blue. This will keep the rest of the design from becoming blue when the cloth is dipped into dye. After the blue parts of the design have been dyed, they will be covered with wax, too. Then workers will carefully scratch the wax off the parts of the

*See Glossary

Making a floor mat in South Vietnam. Handicrafts are very important to the village people of Southeast Asia. Why is this so? What are some of the natural resources used by the craftsmen of this region?

104

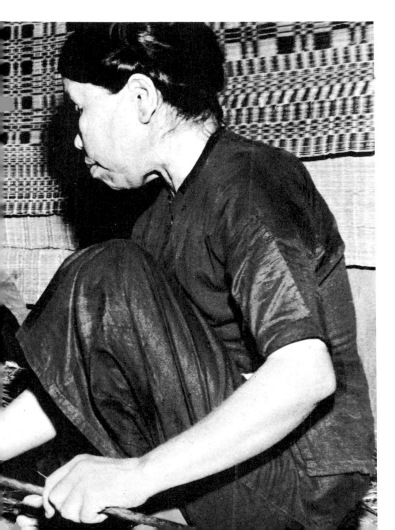

Making batik in Indonesia. This method of decorating fabric requires many different steps. Do research to discover what they are. How can work like this help people meet their needs?

cloth that are to be dyed red. This process will be repeated several times to add still other colors to the pattern. Cloth that is decorated in this way is called batik.

We watch people make other things by hand while we are in Southeast Asia. Metalworkers hammer lovely designs on handmade dishes of copper, aluminum, silver, and gold. Carpenters make farm tools and other useful articles. Many of the things that farm families use are made at home. Men and boys build bamboo fish traps, and women and girls weave fishnets out of twine. Brooms and wooden spoons may also be made at home.

Villagers in Southeast Asia have to make many of the articles they use because they have very little money to spend. Most village people are farmers who produce only enough food for themselves and their families. When they do have anything left over, they may trade it for other things they need at the village market, or sell it to make a little money. Then they may buy a few machine-made goods such as cloth or needles. City people in Southeast Asia buy more machine-made goods than villagers do, for they usually have more money. A large part of the manufactured articles sold in Southeast Asian villages and cities are shipped in from other parts of the world.

Southeast Asia has little modern industry. People in Southeast Asia have to

Using Tools

See pages 137-140

A Problem To Solve
The picture at right shows a worker operating a machine in a tire factory near Bangkok, Thailand. Scenes such as this are not very common in Southeast Asia, however, for there is little modern industry in this region. <u>Why has it been difficult to establish modern industry in this region?</u> In forming hypotheses to solve this problem, you will need to consider how the growth of industry has been affected by the following:
a. the history of Southeast Asia
b. the skills of the people
c. transportation facilities in this region
d. the availability of power to run machines
e. the availability of money and equipment needed to start new factories
Other chapters provide additional information that will be useful in solving this problem.

See Skills Manual, pages 2-4

import many of the machine-made goods they use because there are few factories in the countries of this region. Very little modern industry was developed in these countries before they gained independence. More is now being established, and today we may see some large, modern factories in the cities. However, in most countries of Southeast Asia, fewer than five out of every hundred workers have jobs in factories that are equipped with machinery. Only in a few places, such as Singapore, do a larger proportion of the people earn their living in modern industry.

It is difficult to establish modern industry in the countries of Southeast Asia. The countries in this region usually do not have enough money to pay for buildings and equipment. They lack

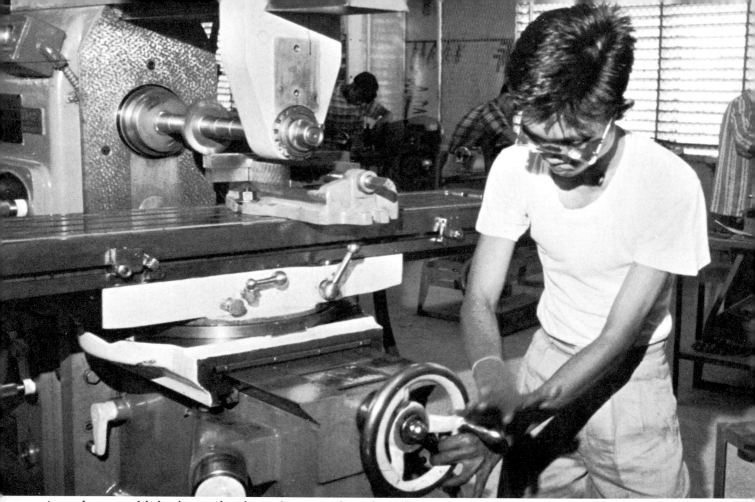

A student machinist in a school run by an Indonesian oil company. Why do you suppose the company set up this school? How do you think attending this school could help the young man meet his needs?

trained factory managers and skilled workers, and they need more electricity to run machines. They also lack many raw materials. In addition, they have too few roads, railroads, trucks, and freight cars to transport goods to and from factories.

Southeast Asian countries are trying to establish more industry. The governments of countries in Southeast Asia are encouraging industry. They try to plan the progress their countries should make to help industry grow. In these plans they decide where new electric power plants are to be built and what improvements are to be made in transportation. In addition, the governments of some countries, such as Burma, plan and run many of the new factories.

Private businessmen are also establishing factories in Southeast Asia. Private industry is especially important in the Philippines, Malaysia, Singapore, and Thailand.

People from other countries are helping Southeast Asian nations to develop more industry. The United Nations, the World Bank, the Ford Foundation, and the Colombo Plan are providing money or other forms of assistance. The governments of the United States, France, Britain, Japan, China, the Soviet Union, and other countries are helping, too. Arrangements have also been made with foreign businessmen to build and run some of the new factories in Southeast Asian countries until the people there learn how to operate them.

The food-processing industry.

The most important industry that the countries of Southeast Asia now have is the preparation of farm products for people to eat. Removing the husks from rice is the main type of food processing. Most Southeast Asian countries have more rice mills than any other kind of mill or factory. Some of the mills are tiny sheds made of corrugated iron. Others are large buildings with modern machinery. Southeast Asia also has sugar mills, bakeries, and soft-drink bottling plants. In addition, there are a few modern fish canneries, as well as smaller establishments where fish are dried or made into sauce.

Preparing raw materials for export.

Another important branch of industry in Southeast Asia is the preparation

Cooperation

See pages 137-140

The workers shown in the picture below are packaging popsicles in a dairy in Thailand. Food processing is Southeast Asia's main industry.

1. Do you think the workers in this dairy need to cooperate with one another? Why? Why not?
2. In what ways does cooperation help people in Southeast Asia to meet their physical needs?

of raw materials for sale to other countries. When we travel through the plantations of this region we may visit smoky sheds where sheets of rubber are being dried. We may also watch workers placing coconut meat in the sun to dry. Other workers prepare tea leaves for export, or work in sawmills. Still others have jobs in tin smelters or petroleum refineries. Each year, more and more of the goods processed in these industries are being used by people in Southeast Asia, instead of being shipped to other countries.

The textile industry. While we are in Southeast Asia we may also watch people making cloth. Some of them work at home, weaving beautiful fabrics on handlooms. Others have jobs in mills equipped with whirring machinery. These mills are usually located in the larger cities. The countries of Southeast Asia need much more cloth than they now produce. Textiles are among the main imports of this region. Raw cotton for the manufacture of textiles is also imported.

The metal industry. Some people in Southeast Asia earn their living in the metal industry. Many of these people have jobs in little workshops where jewelry and other articles are made by hand. Others run machines in small

Baling jute near Khon Kaen, in northeastern Thailand. Many workers in Southeast Asia earn their living by preparing raw materials for export. To what port city do you think this jute will be brought for shipment to other countries? Why do you think this? How might the jute be transported to this city? The maps on pages 8 and 9, 65, and 116 will be useful to you in drawing your conclusions.

Division of Labor

See pages 137–140

The picture at right shows workers assembling an automobile in Thailand.
1. What other kinds of work might people do in an automobile factory?
2. Why do you suppose different workers in this factory have different kinds of jobs?
3. Do you think the division of labor in Thailand and other countries in Southeast Asia is similar to the division of labor in our country? Explain your answer.
Discuss these questions with your classmates.

factories that produce metal goods such as nails, and pots and pans. Some work in assembly plants putting together the parts of cars, bicycles, trucks, or buses that were imported from foreign countries. Still others work in machine shops repairing equipment used in mines, plantations, railroads, and harbors. Several small steel mills have also been established in Southeast Asia, and more are planned.

Other industries. We may visit still other workshops and factories in Southeast Asia. Some of the largest plants produce cement for buildings and roads. Others make tiles and bricks, or manufacture such products as shoes, soap, matches, or rubber tires.

Many people believe that the growth of industry will help Southeast Asia's people achieve a better standard of living. If the right factories are built and properly run, they should provide peo-

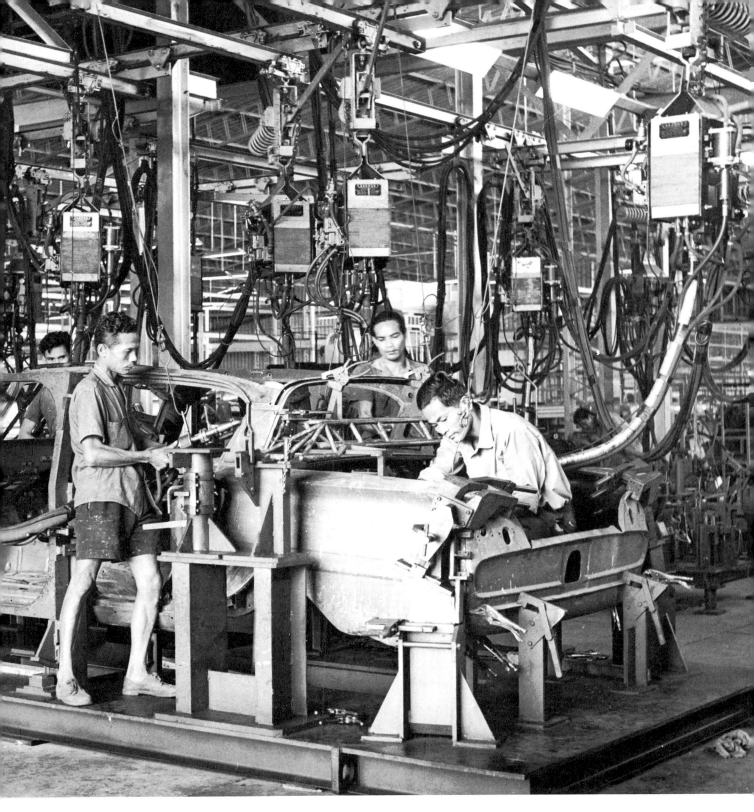

ple with more of the goods they need and want. There should also be more jobs in which people could earn additional money. However, it would be a loss to the world if the establishment of modern factories in Southeast Asia discouraged the fine craftsmen of this region from producing their beautiful batiks and other lovely handmade articles.

13 Transportation and Communication

A boat trip down the Irrawaddy River. We have just boarded a paddle-wheeled steamboat at Bhamo, a town on the Irrawaddy River of Burma. (See the map on page 65.) From here we will travel nearly nine hundred miles to the great city of Rangoon, Burma's most important port. If we were taking a trip on the Irrawaddy during the rainy season, we could start more than a hundred miles farther upstream, because the river would be higher then.

As we move downstream day after day we see hundreds of boats, for the Irrawaddy is Burma's main water highway. Most of the vessels are moved by sails, oars, or poles, but quite a few have steam or diesel engines. To our left is a diesel tug pushing an oil barge. Behind us are several long, canoelike

boats carrying farm products to market. Many of the boats we see belong to the government-owned Inland Water Transport Board.

We are now in the delta of the Irrawaddy. As we near the coast, we turn onto a twenty-two-mile-long canal that links the Irrawaddy River to Rangoon. On both sides of the canal are rice fields that are crisscrossed by streams and other canals. Many of the boats and barges we see on these waterways are carrying rice to markets in Rangoon.

Now we are entering the bustling harbor of Rangoon. The shallow Rangoon River, which links this inland city to the sea, has been dredged deep enough for ocean vessels. We see large ocean freighters here, as well as smaller boats like those we saw on the Irrawaddy. As we pass one freighter we see that it is unloading rolls of newsprint, which will be used to make newspapers. Cloth, automobiles, electric generators, and other goods manufactured in foreign countries are also being unloaded at the

Exchange

See pages 137–140

A Problem To Solve

In the harbor of Rangoon, Burma (left), you can see many kinds of vessels. Some are large oceangoing ships from countries in other parts of the world. Others are small boats that have carried goods from Burmese villages to Rangoon by way of the Irrawaddy River and other waterways. In Burma, as in the other countries of Southeast Asia, goods are also transported from place to place by trucks, trains, and other means of land transportation. All of these forms of transportation are involved in trade. Why is trade important to the people of Southeast Asia? In forming hypotheses to solve this problem, you will need to consider facts about:

1. the natural resources of Southeast Asia
2. farming in this region
3. crafts and industry
4. ways in which people meet their physical needs

See Skills Manual, pages 2–4

115

wharves. Smaller boats will carry some of these goods up the rivers or along the coast to towns in other parts of Burma. To pay for these imported manufactured goods, the freighters will carry away rice, lumber, and minerals. These products were brought to Rangoon in smaller boats from other sections of the country.

Almost every country in Southeast Asia has a main port city like Rangoon, where large ships from other parts of the world may dock. (See the map on page 65.) Southeast Asia's most important port is Singapore. You can read more about this great city on page 63.

Water travel is very important in Southeast Asia. Waterways take the place of roads and railroads in many parts of Southeast Asia. On the Indo-Chinese Peninsula there are several great rivers besides the Irrawaddy, along which boats travel for long distances. Branching off these main water routes are many smaller waterways on which boats

Main roads in Southeast Asia. In some parts of this region, there are no roads at all.

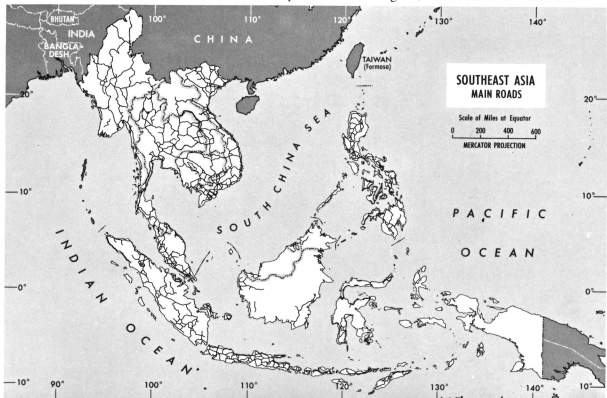

A crowded street in Saigon, South Vietnam. On city streets in Southeast Asia, you can see many different kinds of vehicles. What kinds can you identify in this picture?

also travel. Most of the rivers in the Philippines, Indonesia, and the Malay Peninsula can be used only by small, flat-bottomed boats. However, ships carry goods along the coasts or between the islands in these areas.

Streets and roads. After our visit to the harbor of Rangoon we travel by ship to Bangkok, the capital of Thailand. On a drive through the city we notice that the traffic here is similar to traffic in other large cities of Southeast Asia. As we ride down one of the wide, paved avenues in the center of the city we see many automobiles, trucks, motor scooters, bicycles, and motorcycles. Plodding slowly toward us is a pair of oxen pulling a two-wheeled wooden cart. A little farther down the busy street we see some people carrying large loads on their heads. We also pass several crowded buses.

Later in the afternoon we drive out into the country along one of Thailand's main highways. This is a paved road two lanes wide. Before long we overtake a bus that is traveling from Bangkok to a nearby town. It is packed with people. Bicycles, bundles, and crates of vegetables are strapped on top.

As we go farther along, we frequently pass oxcarts loaded with rice and other farm products. They have probably turned onto the highway from side roads that lead back to farming villages. These village roads are unpaved and are very narrow. During the rainy season many of them are so muddy that they cannot be used.

Thailand and the other countries of Southeast Asia need more good roads. (See the map on page 116.) Many of the roads these countries now have would be more useful if they were paved for all-weather use. Some areas have no roads at all. Often, people in these isolated places have to walk when they wish to travel somewhere, unless there is a waterway nearby.

There are several reasons why Southeast Asia does not have more good roads. The nations here do not have enough money to build all the roads they need. Many of them do not have enough engineers, either. Geographic conditions also cause problems. It is difficult to build roads in many places, for there are steep mountains, and lowlands that are flooded during the rainy season. There are numerous rivers over which bridges must be built. In addition, fast-growing vegetation makes it hard to build roads and keep them in good repair.

Railroads. The same things that make it difficult to build roads in Southeast Asia also make it hard to build railroads. Laos has no railroads at all. In the

A train station on the Indo-Chinese Peninsula. Southeast Asia has few railroads. Most of them are located in the thickly populated lowlands.

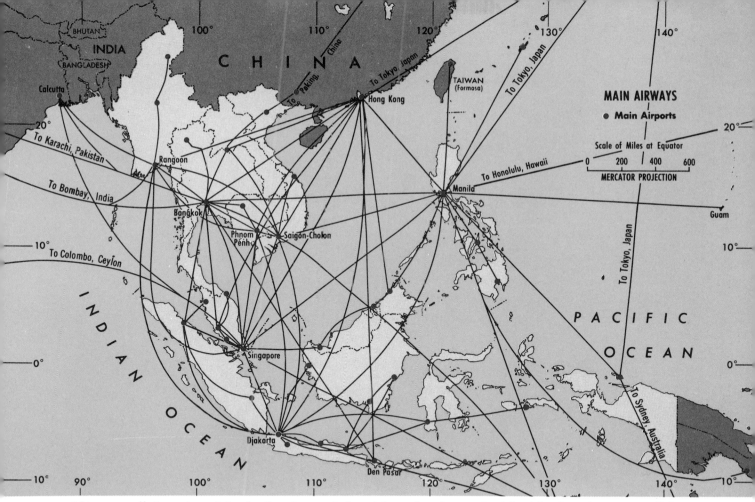

Air routes link major cities in Southeast Asia with each other and with cities in other parts of the world. Airplanes are an especially useful means of transportation in this region. Why is this so?

rest of Southeast Asia, most of the railroads lead from the main cities through the thickly populated coastal lowlands and river plains. The densest rail network is on the island of Java.

Most countries of Southeast Asia are trying to improve their railroads. More and more diesel-electric locomotives are being used, although we may still see locomotives that burn wood or coal. There are some comfortable air-conditioned coaches, but the fare is expensive. Most Southeast Asian people must travel in older cars that are noisy, crowded, and usually hot.

It is important for the countries of Southeast Asia to build more railroads and roads. Until they do, farmers in many parts of this region will not be able to get their produce to market. Improved transportation is also needed in order for industry to grow. (See Chapter 12.)

Air travel. Air travel is especially useful in a region like Southeast Asia where other kinds of transportation are usually poor. Every country in Southeast Asia is served by airlines, with planes that fly to most of the important cities. However, very few people can afford to use these airlines.

Planes from many parts of the world stop in Southeast Asia's large cities on their flights to Europe, Australia, North America, and other parts of Asia. Bangkok is Southeast Asia's most important center of international air traffic. On several main air routes it is exactly halfway around the world from New York City. Bangkok and other important cities such as Singapore, Manila, Djakarta, and Phnom Penh have airports that are large enough for jet planes to land and take off safely.

Communications. In all the large cities of Southeast Asia, and in many of the smaller ones, there are radios, telephones, and newspapers. Some of the cities also have television stations. Many village people do not have radios of their own. However, many community gathering places, such as a village meeting hall, have radios to which people may listen. Radio loudspeakers are also set up in some villages of Southeast Asia.

People in many of the cities and large towns of Southeast Asia may send and receive telegrams and cables. Postal service is provided throughout this region, but in remote areas letters may take a long time to be delivered. Although increasing numbers of people can read and write, news often travels fastest by radio and by people talking to each other in the marketplace.

Passengers leaving a plane at Bangkok's international airport. Several Southeast Asian cities, including Bangkok, Singapore, and Manila, have airports that are large enough to handle jet planes. Bangkok is the chief center of international air traffic in Southeast Asia.

Problems To Solve

As you explore ways of earning a living in Southeast Asia, you may wish to solve one or more of the problems below. (See pages 2-4 of the Skills Manual.)

1. Most farmers in Southeast Asia earn very little money. Why is this so? In solving this problem you will need to make hypotheses about how farm incomes in Southeast Asia are influenced by the following:
   a. the farm methods used here
   b. land ownership and moneylending practices in parts of this region

2. Fish takes the place of meat in the diets of many people in Southeast Asia. Why is this so? In solving this problem you will need to make hypotheses about the following:
   a. the kinds of food available to people in Southeast Asia
   b. religions in Southeast Asia whose teachings influence diet

3. Why is water travel so important in the countries of Southeast Asia? In forming hypotheses to solve this problem, you will need to consider the following:
   a. the climate of this region
   b. the land transportation facilities available to the people of this region
   c. waterways and harbors in this region

Discover the Importance of Rubber

Rubber is one of Southeast Asia's main export products. Prepare a report about rubber that includes the following information:
a. where and how rubber was first used
b. the development of the rubber industry in Europe and the United States, from the 1700's to the present day
c. some uses of rubber in the world today
d. how the development of synthetic rubber has affected the market for natural rubber
The suggestions on pages 12-17 of the Skills Manual will help you prepare a good report.

Investigate the World's Fish Supply

In recent years there has been growing concern about a decrease in the world's supply of fish. Do research and prepare a report about this problem. Your report should include answers to the following questions.

1. In what ways do modern methods of fishing threaten the world's supply of fish?
2. What are some other threats to the world's fish supply?
3. What are some of the most heavily fished areas in the world?
4. What are some of the ways in which the fish supply can be increased?
5. What steps are being taken to increase the supply?

Discuss the Need for Modern Industry

Hold a class debate on the following topic.
Modern factories should be established in Southeast Asian countries even at the expense of discouraging craftsmen who specialize in fine handmade articles.
Both sides will need to consider whether the growth of industry is the only way to improve the standard of living in Southeast Asia.

Learning About Bamboo

One of the most interesting and useful forest products of Southeast Asia is bamboo. Write a report about bamboo that includes the following information:
a. a description of some of the different types of bamboo
b. the parts of the world in which bamboo most commonly grows
c. uses of bamboo
Refer to pages 12-14 of the Skills Manual for help in locating information.

Draw a Map Showing Farm Crops

Draw or trace a large map of Southeast Asia. On your map show the crops that are raised in various parts of this region. You may want to use symbols or colors to identify the different crops. Be sure to include a key box for your map. Chapter 10 provides much of the information you will need. You may also wish to do research in other sources.

Make a Transportation Mural

With a group of your classmates, make a mural showing various kinds of transportation used in Southeast Asian countries. Include the most primitive as well as the most modern.

Part 5
Countries of Southeast Asia

In Part 5 you will be learning more about the countries of Southeast Asia. These countries have much in common, but there are also many differences among them. The fact tables on the following pages will help you make comparisons between individual countries in this region. For example, you may use these tables to help you discover answers to the following questions.

- Which Southeast Asian country is the largest in area? in population? Which is the smallest in area? in population?
- Which country has the highest per capita income? Which has the lowest? What facts do you think help explain the differences in per capita income?

You may also wish to do research in other sources about the history of one or more countries in Southeast Asia. Share your discoveries with your class.

War refugees in South Vietnam. Ever since the end of World War II, the Vietnamese people have been involved in bitter warfare. During this time, serious conflicts have also disrupted other countries of Southeast Asia. You may wish to do research about Vietnam and other countries in this region to discover reasons for these conflicts. In what ways do you think warfare has affected the daily lives of people in Southeast Asia?

Burma

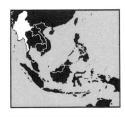

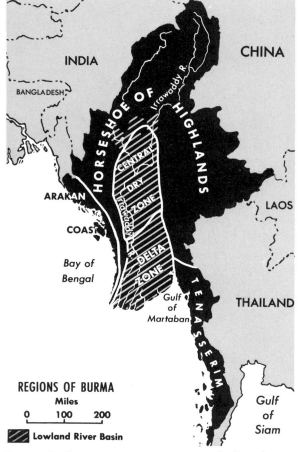

REGIONS OF BURMA

Miles

0   100   200

▨ Lowland River Basin

Burma is the westernmost country in Southeast Asia. The Irrawaddy is Burma's chief river.

Land. Burma is a little smaller than the state of Texas. Most of the country is located on the Indo-Chinese Peninsula, but the southeastern part extends like the tail of a kite into the Malay Peninsula. This section of Burma is called Tenasserim.

A great lowland basin stretches from north to south through the heart of Burma. It is formed of several river valleys separated by low mountains. The main river flowing through this basin is the Irrawaddy, Burma's most important waterway. The northern part of the lowland basin receives less rainfall than the rest of the country. This is

Burma's Central Dry Zone. Farther south the basin spreads into the Delta Zone, which borders the coast.

A horseshoe of forested highlands borders the lowland basin on the east, the west, and the north. Between the western highlands and the sea are the small plains of the Arakan Coast.

Climate. The weather is never very cold in Burma except in the highlands. Most of the rain that falls comes between May and October. From November to January, the weather is cool and dry. In February, March, and April, it is uncomfortably hot and dry.

Facts About Burma

Area: 261,790 square miles.

Population: 28,087,000.

Capital and Largest City: Rangoon (population 1,759,000).

Literacy: About six tenths of the people in Burma can read and write.

Main Religion: Buddhism.

Main Occupation: About seven tenths of the workers are farmers.

Income: Average yearly per capita income is about $77. Though most people in Burma have very little money, they usually raise all the food they need.

Important Farm Products: Burma is one of the world's leading rice exporters. Other important farm products are cotton, sesamum, sorghum, sugarcane, tobacco, pulses, peanuts, millet, and rubber.

Natural Resources: Petroleum, lead, silver, zinc, tin, tungsten, teak trees, and gemstones.

Manufacturing: About seven out of every hundred workers earn their living in industry. Some of them are employed in sugar or rice mills, oil refineries, sawmills, or cement plants. Also, many workers make articles by hand in small workshops or at home.

Currency: Burma's unit of money is the *kyat*, which is officially worth about 19 cents.

Cambodia

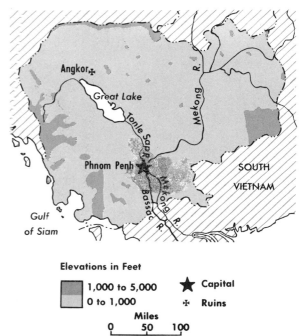

Facts About Cambodia

Area: 69,898 square miles.

Population: 7,000,000.

Capital and Largest City: Phnom Penh. The estimated population of Phnom Penh in 1968 was 600,000. Since then, however, many thousands of war refugees have come to the city.

Literacy: About six tenths of the people can read and write.

Main Religion: Buddhism.

Main Occupation: Nearly nine tenths of the workers earn their living in agriculture.

Income: Average yearly per capita income is about $150. Although most Cambodians have little money to spend, they usually grow enough food for their needs. At village markets, the people trade or sell extra food and handmade articles in order to obtain other things they want.

Important Farm Products: About four fifths of the cropland is planted in rice. Among the other important farm products are rubber, corn, palm sugar, tobacco, and soybeans.

Natural Resources: Fisheries, forests, clay, salt, phosphates, limestone, and gemstones such as sapphires and rubies.

Manufacturing: About two out of every hundred workers are employed in industry. The main kinds of industry here include rice milling and the manufacture of cement and paper. Handicrafts are also important.

Currency: Cambodia's unit of money is the *riel*. About 125 *riel* are officially worth $1.00.

Land. Cambodia, which is about the size of Missouri, is located on the Indo-Chinese Peninsula. Its neighbors to the north and west are Laos and Thailand. To the southeast is South Vietnam, and to the southwest is the Gulf of Siam.

About three fourths of Cambodia consists of a broad, central lowland. In this lowland is the Great Lake. (See map on this page.) During the dry season, the

Cambodia is located on the Indo-Chinese Peninsula. About three fourths of the country consists of a broad lowland area.

Great Lake covers about one thousand square miles and is very shallow. During the rainy season, however, it is about four times as large and much deeper. The central plain of Cambodia is bordered on the east, the north, and the southwest by forested highlands.

The Mekong River and several of its branches flow through the eastern part of Cambodia. This river system and the Great Lake flood much of the central lowland during the rainy season. Each year, their floodwaters deposit a layer of silt over the countryside. The silt helps to enrich the farmlands in central Cambodia.

Climate. The weather in Cambodia is warm throughout the year. The rainy season lasts from June through November, and the dry season from December through May.

Laos

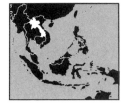

Facts About Laos

Area: 91,429 square miles.

Population: 3,033,000.

Capital and Largest City: Vientiane (population 162,000) is the administrative capital.

Royal Residence: Luang Prabang (population 23,000).

Literacy: About one fifth of the people can read and write.

Main Religion: Buddhism. Animism is practiced along with this religion.

Main Occupation: More than nine tenths of the workers are farmers.

Income: Average yearly per capita income is about $90. Although most of the people in Laos have very little money, they usually grow or make the things they need. They exchange extra food and handmade articles at village markets.

Important Farm Products: Most of the cropland is planted in rice. Corn, coffee, tea, tobacco, cotton, potatoes and other vegetables, peanuts, opium poppies, and livestock are also raised.

Natural Resources: Some forest products, salt, and tin are produced. There are also deposits of other minerals.

Manufacturing: Laos has little modern industry. There are some sawmills, rice mills, and tanneries, and several small factories that make cement, soft drinks, or other goods. Handicrafts are also important in this country.

Currency: Laos' unit of money is the *kip*. About 600 *kip* are officially worth $1.00.

Land. Laos is located on the Indo-Chinese Peninsula. It is about the size of Pennsylvania and New York combined. On the west and northwest, Laos is bordered by Thailand, Burma, and China. To the east are North and South Vietnam, and to the south is Cambodia. The Mekong River forms much of the border between Laos and Thailand. As the map on pages 8-9 shows, Laos is the only country in Southeast Asia that has no seacoast.

Rugged, forested mountains cover a large part of Laos. (See map below.) The country's highest mountain is Mount Bia, which rises more than nine thousand feet above sea level. In the mountains are narrow river valleys in which farming villages are located. The main lowland areas in Laos are the plains that lie along the Mekong River. Vientiane, the capital and largest city of Laos, is located on one of these river plains.

Climate. Except in the mountains, the weather is always warm in Laos. Most of the country receives between fifty and ninety inches of rain each year. The weather is very rainy from May to October, and very dry from November to April.

Laos is the only Southeast Asian country that has no seacoast. In what ways might the lack of a coast affect the country's development?

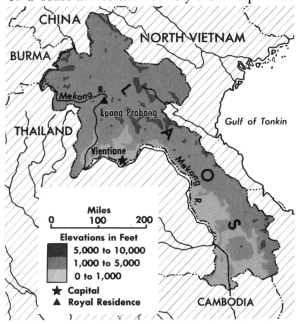

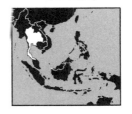

Thailand

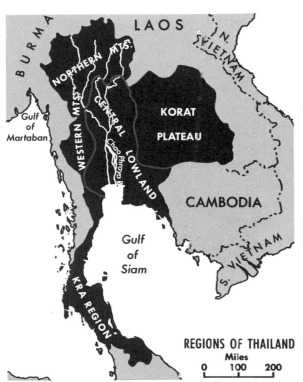

Thailand may be divided into four regions.

Land. Thailand is about the size of France. Most of the country is located on the Indo-Chinese Peninsula. The southern part, however, stretches like a long, curving handle into the Malay Peninsula. Thailand's neighbor on the south is Malaysia. To the west is Burma, and to the east are Laos and Cambodia.

Thailand may be divided into four main regions. (See map above.) In the north and west are mountains. In the northeast is a tableland called the Korat Plateau. Between the mountains and the plateau is the Central Lowland, where most of Thailand's people live. It is formed of the valleys of the Chao Phraya and several other rivers. The part of the Central Lowland near the coast is called the Delta. Thailand's fourth region is the part of the country that extends southward into the Malay Peninsula. This is the Kra Region.

Climate. The temperature seldom falls below sixty-five degrees in Thailand, except in the northern highlands. In most of the country the rainy season lasts from May to October. From October to February the weather is cool and dry. This is followed by hot, dry weather, which lasts until the rains begin again.

Facts About Thailand

Area: 198,457 square miles.

Population: 36,925,000.

Capital and Largest City: Bangkok (population including suburbs about 2,300,000).

Literacy: About seven tenths of Thailand's people can read and write.

Main Religion: Buddhism.

Main Occupation: More than eight tenths of Thailand's workers earn their living by farming.

Income: The average yearly per capita income is about $170. Although most people in Thailand do not have much money to spend, they usually grow enough food for their own needs. At village markets, they exchange extra crops and handmade articles.

Important Farm Products: About four fifths of the farmland in Thailand is planted in rice. Thailand is one of the world's leading rice exporters. Other important farm products are rubber, cassava, sugarcane, tobacco, bananas, corn, and livestock.

Natural Resources: Teak trees, tin, tungsten, and iron ore.

Manufacturing: About four out of every hundred workers in Thailand earn their living in manufacturing. Rice milling is the main branch of industry. There are also sawmills, sugar mills, textile mills, and a tin smelter. Handicrafts are produced in workshops and homes.

Currency: Thailand's unit of money is the *baht*. Twenty-one *baht* are officially worth about $1.00.

Vietnam – Two Countries

Since 1954, Vietnam has been divided into two countries, North Vietnam and South Vietnam. (See map below.) A brief summary of Vietnam's history will help you understand why this division took place.

1. <u>300 B.C.–A.D. 939.</u> In the third century B.C., a kingdom was established in the northern part of the area today called Vietnam. The Chinese took over this kingdom in 111 B.C. and ruled it until A.D. 939, when the Vietnamese regained their independence.

2. <u>A.D. 939–1800.</u> Over several hundred years, the Vietnamese gradually occupied much of Cambodia and what is now South Vietnam. By the late 1700's their control extended into the Mekong Delta. At that time, Vietnam was ruled by an emperor. However, two rival families—one in the northern part of the country and the other in the south—held the real power.

3. <u>1800-1941.</u> French missionaries and traders had come to Vietnam in the 1600's. During the 1800's France gradually gained control of Vietnam and in 1887 made it part of French Indochina. In the early 1900's, many Vietnamese began to work for independence. One of their leaders was Ho Chi Minh.* In 1941, he formed the Vietnamese Independence League, or Vietminh. The main leaders of this organization were Communists.

4. <u>1941-1954.</u> During World War II, the Vietminh continued the struggle for independence. By 1945 it had an army of about ten thousand soldiers and had gained much power in northern Vietnam. In 1945, after Japan surrendered, the Vietminh quickly took over the government of Vietnam and declared the country independent. Soon fighting broke out between the French and the Vietnamese in southern Vietnam. The Vietminh again led the struggle for independence. Fighting continued until 1954, when the French forces were defeated. In that year, at a conference in Geneva, Switzerland, Vietnam was divided near the 17th parallel. The northern part of the country was to be governed by the Communist Vietminh, and the southern part by France.

5. <u>1955-present.</u> In 1955, South Vietnam became independent. Two years later, Communist guerrillas began to wage war against the government of South Vietnam. This war, which eventually involved the United States and several other countries, is still going on. Pages 44-45 explain more about this war.

*See Glossary

Vietnam is divided into two countries.

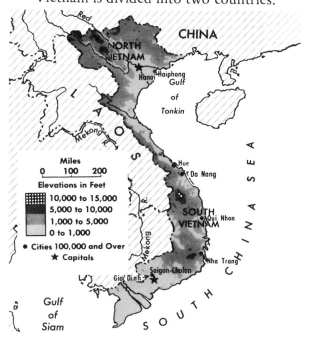

Land. Although North Vietnam and South Vietnam are separate countries, we may consider the area they occupy as a geographical unit called Vietnam. Vietnam extends along the eastern coast of the Indo-Chinese Peninsula. (Compare the map on the opposite page with the map on page 2.)

Vietnam has rugged highlands and fertile lowlands. The most important lowlands are the deltas of the Red and Mekong rivers. Along the coast between these deltas are many small plains. The highlands of Vietnam are located behind these plains and in the north.

Climate. Vietnam's climate varies considerably from north to south. In the south, the weather is warm all year round. In the north, temperatures are about twenty degrees cooler in winter than in summer. However, except in the highlands, winters in the north are still warm enough for crops to grow. Although the average yearly rainfall is heavy, the amount differs from year to year, especially in the north.

Facts About South Vietnam

Area: 65,948 square miles.

Population: 18,000,000.

Capital and Largest City: Saigon (population, with Cholon, 2,000,000).

Literacy: About six tenths of the people can read and write.

Main Religions: Buddhism, Taoism, Confucianism, Christianity Caodaism, and Hoa Hao. Animism and ancestor worship are also practiced.

Main Occupation: About three fourths of the working people earn their living in agriculture.

Income: Average yearly per capita income is about $130. Although South Vietnam's people have little money to spend, they raise most of the food they need. They exchange extra food and handmade articles at village markets.

Important Farm Products: In normal times, large amounts of rice and rubber are exported. Rice is the main food crop. Other important farm products are corn, copra, sugarcane, tobacco, cassava, peanuts, pepper, and sweet potatoes.

Natural Resources: Forests, fisheries, waterpower, gold, and some low-grade coal.

Manufacturing: South Vietnam has little modern industry. However, there is an increasing number of factories that produce cloth, matches, soap, or other goods. Handicrafts and the processing of farm and forest products are important.

Currency: South Vietnam's unit of money is the *piastre*. About 400 *piastre* are officially worth $1.00.

Facts About North Vietnam

Area: 61,293 square miles.

Population: 21,200,000.

Capital and Largest City: Hanoi (population 643,600).

Literacy: The North Vietnamese government reports that more than nine tenths of the people can read and write.

Main Religions: Buddhism, Taoism, Confucianism, and Christianity. Animism and ancestor worship are also practiced.

Main Occupation: About three fourths of the working people earn their living in agriculture.

Income: Average yearly per capita income is about $90. Most of North Vietnam's farm families belong to agricultural cooperatives. Some workers earn part of their living from handicrafts.

Important Farm Products: Rice is the main crop. Other farm products are sugarcane, corn, cotton, tea, coffee, tobacco, castor oil, and sweet potatoes and other vegetables. Mulberry leaves are also raised as food for silkworms.

Natural Resources: Coal, phosphates, salt, tin, chromite, iron, zinc, tungsten, manganese, forests, fisheries, and waterpower.

Manufacturing: North Vietnam has more factories than South Vietnam. Food processing and the manufacture of textiles are the leading industries. Handicrafts are also important.

Currency: North Vietnam's unit of money is the *dong*. One *dong* is officially worth about 34 cents.

Malaysia

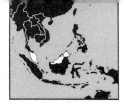

The country of Malaysia is a federation of thirteen states. Eleven of these are located on the Malay Peninsula, and formerly were known as the Federation of Malaya. The other two states, Sarawak and Sabah, are located on the island of Borneo and were once under British control. Before Sabah became part of Malaysia, it was known as North Borneo.

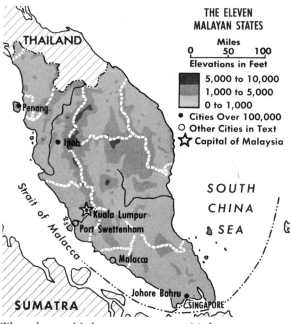

The eleven Malayan states, or Malaya, are part of a country called the Federation of Malaysia.

The Eleven Malayan States

Land. Malaya is a little larger than New York. It occupies the southern part of the Malay Peninsula and several small islands. To the north is Thailand. On the west the Strait of Malacca separates Malaya from the island of Sumatra. Off the southern coast is Singapore.

Forested mountain ranges stretch from north to south through Malaya. Along the eastern and western coasts are lowlands. Only a small part of the eastern coastal lowlands has been cleared. Most of the farms, mines, and cities are on the western coastal lowlands. Much of Malaya is still covered with forests and swamps.

Climate. Except in the highlands, the weather in Malaya is hot and humid throughout the year. Almost everywhere the annual rainfall is more than seventy inches. Rain falls during every month, but some seasons are rainier than others.

Facts About the Eleven Malayan States

Area: About 50,700 square miles.

Population: 9,500,000.

Capital and Largest City of Malaysia: Kuala Lumpur (population 592,800).

Literacy: Nearly half of the people can read and write.

Main Religions: Islam is the official religion, but there are also many Buddhists, Confucianists, Taoists, Hindus, and Christians.

Main Occupation: About half of the workers earn their living by farming. Many of these people have jobs on plantations.

Income: Average yearly per capita income is about $330.

Important Farm Products: Two thirds of the cropland is planted in rubber trees. Coconuts, palm oil, pineapples, and tea are also produced for export. Rice is the main food crop.

Natural Resources: Malaya is the world's largest producer of tin. Other important natural resources are iron, gold, bauxite, forests, and fisheries.

Manufacturing: The processing of raw materials, such as rubber and tin, is the main branch of industry. There are some factories that make petroleum products, food products, cement, rubber goods, or other products. Handicrafts are important, also.

Currency: Malaya's unit of money is the Malaysian dollar. It is officially worth about 35 cents.

Sarawak, Sabah, and Brunei

Sarawak, Sabah, and Brunei are three territories on the island of Borneo. Until 1963, all three of these territories were under British control. In that year, Sarawak and Sabah became part of Malaysia. Brunei chose not to join Malaysia, and is still a British protectorate.

Although Brunei is much smaller than Sarawak and Sabah, it is very important. More oil is produced in this small territory than in any other part of Southeast Asia except Indonesia.

Most of the land along the coasts of Sarawak, Sabah, and Brunei is low and swampy. Farther inland are many mountains. Rainforests cover about three fourths of the land. The weather is hot and rainy the year around.

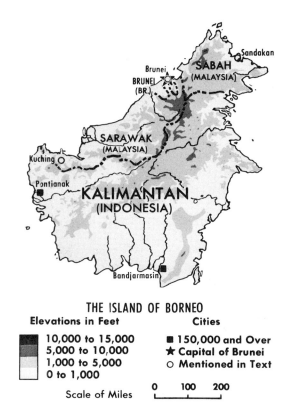

THE ISLAND OF BORNEO

Elevations in Feet

- 10,000 to 15,000
- 5,000 to 10,000
- 1,000 to 5,000
- 0 to 1,000

Cities

- ■ 150,000 and Over
- ★ Capital of Brunei
- ○ Mentioned in Text

Scale of Miles   0   100   200

	Sarawak	Sabah	Brunei
Political Status	State in the Federation of Malaysia.	State in the Federation of Malaysia.	British-protected sultanate.
Area	48,250 square miles.	29,388 square miles.	2,226 square miles.
Population	1,019,000.	691,000.	129,000.
Largest City	Kuching (population 70,000).	Sandakan (population 33,300).	Brunei, capital (population 34,000).
Main Religions	Islam, Buddhism, Christianity, animism.	Islam, Buddhism, Christianity, animism.	Islam, Buddhism, animism.
Important Farm Products	Rice, rubber, sago, pepper, coconuts.	Rubber, rice, sago, coconuts, manioc, abaca, tobacco.	Rubber, rice, sago, coconuts.
Natural Resources	Petroleum, bauxite, gold, phosphate, coal, forests.	Forests, fisheries.	Petroleum, forests.
Industry	Oil refining, lumbering, processing rubber and other raw materials for export, handicrafts.	Lumbering, processing rubber and other raw materials for export, handicrafts.	Oil drilling, processing rubber and other raw materials for export, handicrafts.
Currency	Malaysian dollar.	Malaysian dollar.	Brunei dollar, worth about 30 cents.

The Philippines

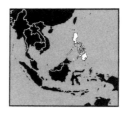

Facts About the Philippines

Area: The Philippines is made up of about 7,100 islands, which together form a land area of 115,830 square miles.

Population: 39,906,000.

Capital: Quezon City (population 545,500).

Largest City: Manila (population 1,550,000).

Literacy: About three fourths of the people in the Philippines can read and write.

Main Religion: Christianity, predominantly Roman Catholicism.

Main Occupation: Three fifths of the workers earn their living by farming.

Income: Average yearly per capita income is about $182.

Important Farm Products: The Philippines is the world's largest producer of coconuts and abaca, which are raised mainly for export. Cane sugar and tobacco are other important export products. For their own use, farmers raise rice, corn, sweet potatoes, beans, peas, and fruit.

Natural Resources: Copper, iron, chromite, gold, manganese, forests, fisheries, and waterpower.

Manufacturing: The processing of foods and the preparation of farm products for export are the main kinds of manufacturing. Cement, textiles, paper, plywood, soap, drugs, and many other goods are also manufactured.

Currency: The Philippines' unit of money is the *peso*, which is officially worth about 16 cents.

Harvesting rice on Negros, one of the eleven largest islands of the Philippines. This country includes more than seven thousand islands.

Land. The Philippines is an archipelago of about 7,100 islands located east of the Indo-Chinese Peninsula. This island country is about the size of the state of Arizona.

The eleven largest islands of the Philippines include more than nine tenths of the land area. These islands are Luzon, Mindanao, Palawan, Samar, Negros, Panay, Mindoro, Leyte, Cebu, Bohol, and Masbate. (See map at right.) You can read more about the land of the Philippines in Chapter 1.

Climate. Except in the highlands, the weather is warm all year round in the Philippines. Total yearly rainfall varies from 40 inches to 180 inches in different parts of the country. (See the large map on page 20.) You can read more about the climate of the Philippines in Chapter 2.

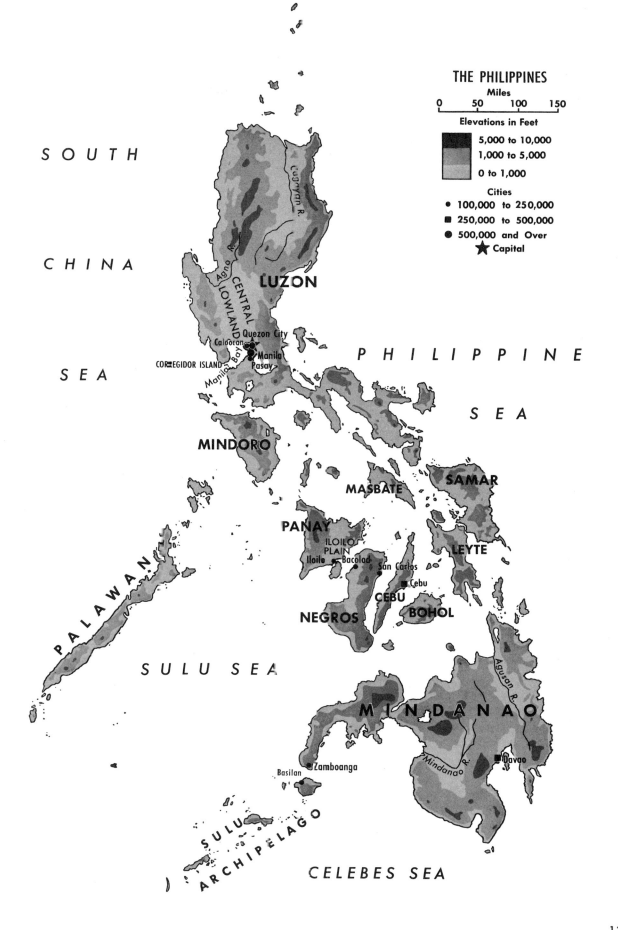

THE PHILIPPINES

Miles

0   50   100   150

Elevations in Feet

5,000 to 10,000
1,000 to 5,000
0 to 1,000

Cities

• 100,000 to 250,000
■ 250,000 to 500,000
● 500,000 and Over
★ Capital

SOUTH

CHINA

SEA

LUZON

Cagayan R.

Agno R.

CENTRAL LOWLAND

Quezon City

Caloocan

Manila

Pasay

CORREGIDOR ISLAND

Manila Bay

PHILIPPINE

SEA

MINDORO

MASBATE

SAMAR

PANAY

ILOILO PLAIN

Iloilo   Bacolod   San Carlos

Cebu

CEBU

LEYTE

NEGROS

BOHOL

PALAWAN

SULU SEA

MINDANAO

Agusan R.

Mindanao R.

Basilan   Zamboanga

Davao

SULU

ARCHIPELAGO

CELEBES SEA

Indonesia

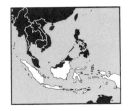

Facts About Indonesia

Area: Indonesia, the largest country in Southeast Asia, has a land area of 735,272 square miles.

Population: 122,043,000.

Capital and Largest City: Djakarta (population 4,774,000).

Literacy: About one half of the people in Indonesia can read and write.

Main Religion: Islam.

Main Occupation: About three fourths of Indonesia's workers are farmers.

Income: Average yearly per capita income is about $95. Although most Indonesians who work on small farms have little money, they usually grow enough food for their families and exchange extra crops and handmade articles at village markets for other things they need. Plantation workers have become unionized since World War II and make a better living than they used to, but still must go without some things they need. Many city people are very poor.

Important Farm Products: Rice, corn, cassava, fruits, sweet potatoes and other vegetables, peanuts, and soybeans are raised for food. Important export products are rubber, tobacco, copra, palm oil, coffee, tea, pepper, cinchona, cacao, kapok, and sisal.

Natural Resources: Petroleum, tin, coal, bauxite, manganese, nickel, forests, and fish.

Manufacturing: Handicrafts and the processing of farm products are the main kinds of manufacturing in Indonesia. In addition, there are shipyards, oil refineries, assembly shops, and factories that produce tires, glass, cement, textiles, soap, or other goods.

Currency: Indonesia's unit of money is the *rupiah*. About 417 *rupiah* are officially worth $1.00.

Land. The island country of Indonesia is located along the equator between the continents of Asia and Australia. It extends about three thousand miles from east to west. The country includes parts of Borneo and New Guinea and about three thousand other islands. Altogether, the land area of Indonesia is nearly three times as large as the state of Texas.

Most of the islands that make up Indonesia are small. The largest islands that lie entirely within the country are Sumatra, Sulawesi, and Java. The part of Borneo that belongs to Indonesia is called Kalimantan. (See map on opposite page.) Western New Guinea, which also belongs to Indonesia, is called West Irian. (See map on pages 8 and 9.)

Climate. The islands of Indonesia lie both north and south of the equator. Except in the high mountains, these islands have warm weather throughout the year. Most of Indonesia receives plenty of rain. In much of the country there are periods of greater and lesser rainfall. Only a part of southeastern Indonesia has a distinct dry season.

Rice fields on the island of Bali. Indonesia is made up of about three thousand islands.

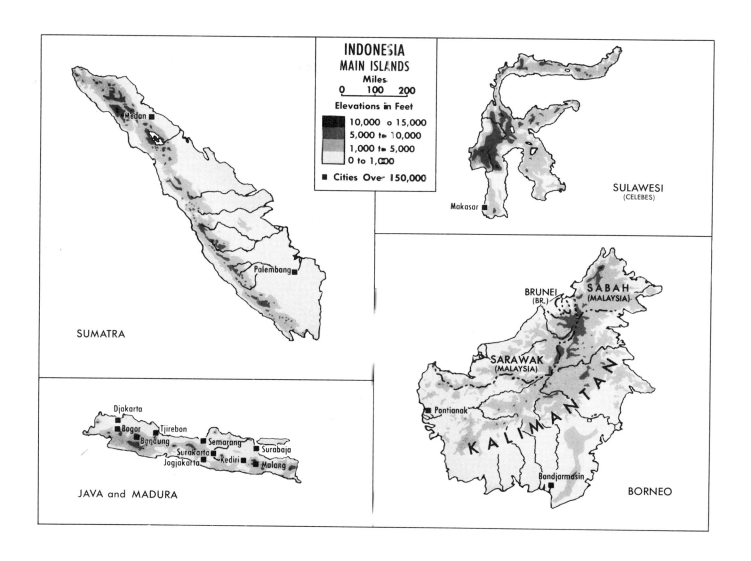

Island	Area	Population	Some Important Facts
Java (including the small neighboring island of Madura)	51,032 square miles	80,187,000	Java, Indonesia's most densely populated island, has much of the country's cultivated land. Most of the people here are farmers who live in permanent villages and raise rice as a main crop. In the uplands are plantations that produce agricultural exports such as rubber and tea.
Sumatra	182,859 square miles	20,378,000	Sumatra produces a large share of Indonesia's exports. Many people here work on plantations or have jobs in the petroleum or fishing industries. Large numbers still farm in temporary forest clearings.
Sulawesi (Celebes)	72,987 square miles	9,167,000	Sulawesi produces rice and some export crops such as coconuts in the northeastern and southwestern parts of the island. In the mountains people farm in temporary clearings. On the coasts, many people are fishermen or traders.
Kalimantan (Indonesian Borneo)	208,286 square miles	5,312,000	Much of Kalimantan is a wilderness inhabited only by tribesmen. Some oil wells, farms, mines, and towns are located along the coast and near navigable rivers.

Singapore

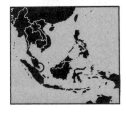

Singapore's land area is only 224 square miles.

Facts About Singapore

Area: Singapore Island and its small neighboring islands together form a land area of 224 square miles.

Population: 2,128,000.

Capital: Singapore (population 2,033,000).

Main Groups of People: Three fourths of the people are Chinese. There are also many Malays and Indians. Fewer than two out of every hundred people are Eurasians or Westerners.

Literacy: About three fourths of the people can read and write.

Main Religions: Buddhism, Confucianism, Taoism, Islam, Hinduism, and Christianity.

Occupations: More than one third of Singapore's workers have jobs in manufacturing. Others work at wharves, warehouses, and businesses that import and re-export goods. Still others are construction workers or have jobs that offer services to other people. Most of the people who live outside the city are farmers or fishermen.

Income: Average yearly per capita income is about $796.

Manufacturing: Building and repairing ships, and processing raw materials such as tin, rubber, and petroleum are the main kinds of manufacturing. There are a few large factories, and many smaller ones that produce soap, soft drinks, cigarettes, vegetable oils, rubber shoes, or other goods.

Currency: Singapore's unit of money is the Singapore dollar. It is officially worth about 35 cents.

Land and climate. Singapore is made up of one main island and about forty tiny, neighboring islands. It is located close to the southern coast of Malaya. A causeway connects Singapore Island to the mainland. Low hills cover much of the island. The highest hill rises 581 feet above sea level. Singapore's climate is hot and rainy all year round.

Processing raw materials such as rubber and tin is a main kind of manufacturing in Singapore.

Great Ideas

of Man

A family in Thailand. A family is one kind of community. In what ways do you think the members of this family use the nine "great ideas" discussed in these pages? Why do you think this? How do you suppose the use of these ideas helps the members of a family meet their needs?

Man has probably been living on the earth for more than two million years. During this time, man has met his needs in communities. No person can meet his needs by himself. Only by living and working with other people can he have a happy, satisfying life.

In order to make community life successful, man has developed certain ideas and ways of living. We call these the "great ideas of man." Let us examine nine of these great ideas and see how they have made it possible for man to live in communities.

Cooperation. In every community, people need to work together in order to accomplish their goals. Working together is called cooperation. Long ago, when most people were hunters, they had to cooperate closely to protect themselves from wild beasts and to get the food they needed. In what ways is cooperation important to communities today? What are some of the ways in which people cooperate with each other? What might happen to a community if people were not willing to work together?

Rules and government. Every community needs rules to guide the ways in which people act toward one another. Why is this true? What kinds of rules does your own community have? How do these rules make life safer and more pleasant for everyone? What would it be like to live in a community in which no one obeyed the rules?

In every community, there must be a person or a group of persons to make the rules and see that they are carried out. In other words, all communities need some form of government. In what ways are all governments alike? How do governments differ from each other?

Language. In order to live and work together, people must be able to express their ideas and feelings to one another. The most important ways of communicating are by speaking and writing. Scientists believe that all human beings—even those who lived in earliest times—have had some form of spoken language. Writing was not developed until about five thousand years ago.

How does language help you to meet your needs? What would you do if you could neither speak nor write? Would you be able to think and to solve problems without using language? Explain your answer.

Education. Another great idea of man is education. In every community, the older people pass on certain ideas and skills to the younger people. Would it be possible to have a successful community without education? Why? Why not?

In early times, parents taught their children most of the things they needed to know in order to live successfully. Today, children in most parts of the world obtain a large part of their education in school. Do you think education is important for every person? Why do you think as you do?

Using natural resources. In order to meet their needs, people in all communities make use of soil, water, air, sunshine, wild plants and animals, and minerals. These gifts of nature are called natural resources. Would a person be able to

Schoolchildren in Burma. About one third of Burma's people cannot read and write. To help solve this problem, the government of Burma is building more schools and holding special classes for adults. Why do you suppose the government is trying to help more people learn to read and write?

meet his needs for food, clothing, and shelter without using natural resources? Why? Why not?

In early times, people made little use of the natural resources around them. Today we use hundreds of natural resources in many different ways. How have changes in the use of natural resources affected your life?

Using tools. A tool is anything that a person uses to help him do work. What kinds of tools do you use every day? In all communities, people use tools in meeting their physical needs. Would it be possible to have a successful community without tools? Why do you think this?

Tools that have a number of moving parts are called machines. Three hundred years ago, most machines were very simple. Then people began to develop more complicated machines. These could do many jobs that had formerly been done by hand. Today people use many different kinds of machines to produce goods. How do modern machines help people to meet their needs more successfully?

Division of labor. In every community, not all the people do exactly the same kinds of work. Instead, they work at different jobs. For example, one man may earn his living by farming. Another man may be a baker and another may be a carpenter. Dividing up the work of a community among people who do different jobs is known as division of labor.

By using division of labor, people are able to obtain more goods than they could if each person tried to meet all of his needs by himself. What do you think are the reasons for this? Would it be

A laboratory worker on a Malaysian rubber plantation. What kind of work do you think this man does? What other kinds of work do you suppose are done on this rubber plantation? Do you think the plantation could be operated successfully without division of labor? Give reasons for your answer.

possible to have a successful community without division of labor? Why? Why not?

Exchange. Whenever people divide up the work of a community, they need to exchange goods and services with each other. In this way, each person is able to obtain goods and services that he does not produce himself. What would it be like to live in a community where people did not use the great idea of exchange?

In early times, people did not carry on as much exchange, or trade, as people do today. We not only exchange goods and services within our own communities but we also carry on trade with people who live in communities far away. Do you think trade helps people everywhere to have a better life? Why do you think this?

Loyalty. In every truly successful community, most of the people are loyal to each other. They are loyal to the laws of their community and their country. They are also loyal to certain ideas and beliefs. In the United States, for example, most people are loyal to the principles of democracy. In addition, many people are loyal to their religious faith.

To what persons and ideas are you loyal? What are some of the ways in which you express your loyalty? How does loyalty help you to meet your needs?

On the docks in Bangkok, Thailand. Trade with other nations is very important to the people of Southeast Asia. Why is this so? In what ways does this kind of exchange help people meet their needs?

The Needs of Man

The people of Southeast Asia, like all other people on the earth, must meet certain basic needs in order to be healthy and happy. Scientists who study human behavior tell us that these basic needs are almost exactly the same for every person, whatever his skin color, his national origin, or his religion may be. Whether people are rich or poor, they have the same basic needs.

There are three kinds of basic needs. They are: physical needs, social needs, and the need for faith.

Physical Needs

Some basic needs are so important that people will die or become seriously ill if they fail to meet them. These are called physical needs. They include the need for:

1. air
2. water
3. food
4. protection from heat and cold
5. sleep and rest
6. exercise

Although all people on the earth share these needs, they do not all meet them in the same way. How do you meet your physical needs? How do you suppose people in Southeast Asia meet these needs?

Social Needs

Each person also has social needs. He must meet these needs in order to have a happy and useful life. Man's social needs include the following:

1. Belonging to a group. Every person needs to feel he belongs to a group of people who respect him and whom he respects. Belonging to a family is one of the main ways people meet this need. What can the members of a family do to show that they love and respect each other? How do the members of your family help one another? Do you think family life is important to the people of Southeast Asia? Give reasons for your answer.

Having friends also helps people meet their need for belonging to a group. What groups of friends do you have? Why are these people your friends? Do you think young people in Southeast Asia enjoy doing the same kinds of things with their friends? What makes you think this?

2. Goals. To be happy, every person needs goals to work for. What goals do you have? How can working toward these goals help you have a happy life? Do you think young people in Southeast Asia have goals similar to yours? Give reasons for your answer.

3. A chance to think and learn. Every person needs a chance to develop and use his abilities. He needs opportunities to find out about things that make him curious. What would you like to learn? How can you learn these things? How can developing your abilities help you have a happy life? Is it important for people in Southeast Asia to have a chance to think, learn, and make decisions for themselves? Give reasons for your answer.

4. A feeling of accomplishment. You share with every other person the need for a feeling of accomplishment. Everyone needs to feel that his life is successful in some way. Give examples of times when you have had a feeling of accomplishment. Can you imagine what a person's life would be like if he never had this feeling?

The Need for Faith

In addition to physical and social needs, every person also has a need for faith. He needs to believe that life is precious and that the future is something to look forward to. A person may have different kinds of faith, including the following.

1. Faith in himself. In order to feel secure, each person must have faith in his own abilities. He must feel that he will be able to do some useful work in the world and that he will be generally happy. He must believe that he can work toward solving whatever problems life brings to him. What are some ways in which a person can build faith in himself?

2. Faith in other people. Every person needs to feel that he can count on other people to do their part and to help him when he needs help. What people do you have faith in? What do you think life would be like without this kind of faith?

3. Faith in nature's laws. Another kind of faith that helps people face the future with confidence is faith in nature's laws. The more we learn about our universe, the more certain we feel that we can depend on nature. How would you feel if you couldn't have faith in nature's laws?

4. Religious faith. Throughout history, almost all human beings have had some kind of religious faith. Religion can help people understand themselves and the world they live in. It can bring them joy, and it can give them confidence in times of trouble. Religion can also help people live together happily. For example, most religions teach people to be honest and to love and help their neighbors. In what ways do people in Southeast Asia express their religious faith?

Many People in Southeast Asia Are Unable To Meet Their Basic Needs

The 290 million people living in Southeast Asia must meet the three kinds of basic needs we have explored here. They must meet these needs in order to have happy, useful lives. However, millions of Southeast Asia's people do not have a chance to satisfy some of their important needs. For example, large numbers of them do not have enough food to eat or adequate shelter.

Why are so many people in Southeast Asia unable to meet all of their needs? What is being done to help these people have a better life? Do research in this book and other sources to find information that will help you answer these questions.

142

GLOSSARY

Complete Pronunciation Key

The pronunciation of each word is shown just after the word, in this way: **equator** (i kwā´-tər). The letters and signs used are pronounced as in the words below. The mark ´ is placed after a syllable with a primary or strong accent, as in the example above. The mark ´ after a syllable shows a secondary or lighter accent, as in **hydroelectricity** (hī´ drō i lek´ tris´ ə tē).

a	hat, cap	j	jam, enjoy	u	cup, butter
ā	age, face	k	kind, seek	u̇	full, put
ã	care, air	l	land, coal	ü	rule, move
ä	father, far	m	me, am	ū	use, music
		n	no, in		
		ng	long, bring		
b	bad, rob				
ch	child, much	o	hot, rock	v	very, save
d	did, red	ō	open, go	w	will, woman
		ô	order, all	y	young, yet
e	let, best	oi	oil, voice	z	zero, breeze
ē	equal, see	ou	house, out	zh	measure, seizure
ėr	term, learn				
		p	paper, cup		
f	fat, if	r	run, cry	ə	represents:
g	go, bag	s	say, yes	a	in about
h	he, how	sh	she, rush	e	in taken
		t	tell, it	i	in pencil
i	it, pin	th	thin, both	o	in lemon
ī	ice, five	ŦH	then, smooth	u	in circus

---

abaca´ (ä´ bə kä´). A fiber obtained from the leaf stems of the abaca plant, which is related to the banana plant. Used to make rope.

Allies (al´īz). See **World War II.**

ancestor worship. A form of religion whose followers worship the spirits of their ancestors.

Angkor (ang´ kôr). A group of ruins near the northwestern end of the Great Lake, in Cambodia. (See map, page 65.) Angkor was the capital city of the Khmer Empire. Angkor Wat, a great Khmer temple, is located here. See **Khmers.**

animism (an´ ə miz əm). The belief that objects such as stones and trees possess spirits. People who believe in animism offer prayers and sacrifices to these spirits.

Annam (ə nam´). Former name for the territory now occupied by North and South Vietnam. Under French control, this territory was divided into three parts, and the name Annam referred to the central part.

appreciation. The understanding or awareness of the worth of something. For example, you may develop an appreciation for art or music. You may also develop an appreciation for the accomplishments of people of other cultures.

Arab (ar´ əb). A people whose ancestors originally lived in Arabia.

Arabia (ə rā´ bē ə). A large peninsula in southwestern Asia occupied mainly by the country of Saudi Arabia.

archipelago (är´ kə pel´ə gō). Either a body of water that is dotted with islands, or a group of islands.

Association of Southeast Asian Nations. Also called ASEAN. An organization formed in 1967 by Thailand, the Philippines, Malaysia, Indonesia, and Singapore to promote closer economic and cultural relations among nations in Southeast Asia.

Bagan Siapiapi (bä′gän sē′ä pi ä′pi). A fishing town in eastern Sumatra, located on the Strait of Malacca. (See map, page 65.)

Bahasa (bä hä′sə) **Indonesia**. The official language of Indonesia. It is a new language, based on the Indonesian form of the Malay language.

Bandung (bän′dùng). A large city located in the highlands of western Java, in Indonesia. (See map, page 65.)

Bangka (bang′kə). An island off the southeastern coast of Sumatra, in Indonesia. (See map, pages 8 and 9.) One of the world's leading tin-producing areas.

Bangkok (bang′kok). The capital and largest city of Thailand. (See map, page 65.)

bauxite (bôk′sīt). An ore from which aluminum is obtained.

bazaar (bə zär′). In Asia and Africa, a marketplace or group of shops.

Borneo (bôr′nē ō). An island in the archipelago of Indonesia. The southern two thirds of the island, called Kalimantan, belongs to Indonesia. The rest is divided between Malaysia and the British protectorate of Brunei. (See map, page 131.)

British Commonwealth. See **Commonwealth of Nations**.

Brunei (brù nī′). A sultanate on the island of Borneo, under British protection. (See map, page 131.) See **sultanate**.

Buddhism (bùd′iz əm). A religion founded by Siddhartha Gautama Buddha, who lived in India about 2,500 years ago. Buddha taught that selfishness is the cause of all sorrow, and that brotherly love among all men is the way to happiness.

Burma (ber′mə). An independent country, most of which is located on the Indo-Chinese Peninsula. (Compare map on page 2 with map on pages 8 and 9.)

cabinet. In government, the group of advisors that helps the country's leader make decisions and establish policies. Members of the cabinet are usually administrators in charge of government departments.

cable. In communications, a rope made of wires that is laid underwater to send telephone and telegraph messages overseas. Also, a message sent this way.

cacao (kə kā′ō). Seeds from which chocolate is made. Also, the tree that produces these seeds.

Cagayan (kä′gä yän′) **River**. A river 220 miles long in the northern part of Luzon, in the Philippines.

Calicut (kal′ə kut). A port city in southern India. (See map, page 35.)

Cambodia (kam bō′dē ə). An independent country located in the southeastern part of the Indo-Chinese Peninsula. (Compare map on page 2 with map on pages 8 and 9.)

Cao Dai (kou′ dī′). An organization that follows the religion of Caodaism, founded about forty-five years ago in the territory now called South Vietnam. Caodaism combines ideas from Buddhism, Taoism, Confucianism, and Christianity. Is headed by a pope.

capital. The term used to describe any kind of wealth that is used to produce additional wealth. Includes land, money, factory buildings and machines, power plants, railroads, and steamships.

cassava (kə sä′və). Also called manioc. Any one of several tropical plants with roots that look somewhat like sweet potatoes. The roots of one kind of cassava, called bitter cassava, are poisonous when raw, but are cooked and processed to make tapioca.

causeway. A raised way across low-lying ground, marshy land, or water.

Cebu (sā bü′). One of the eleven main islands in the Philippines. Also, the largest city on this island. (See map, page 133.)

Celebes (sel′ə bēz). See **Sulawesi**.

centimeter. A measure of length in the metric system. Two and one-half centimeters are equal to about one inch.

Ceylon (si lon′). An island in the Indian Ocean close to the southern tip of India. (See map, pages vi-vii.) It is an independent country.

Chao Phraya (chou prī′ə). The most important river in Thailand. Formed where two other rivers from the mountains of northern Thailand join together, about 160 miles from the sea. (See map, pages 8 and 9.)

China. The huge country that occupies about one fifth of Asia. (See map, pages vi-vii.) Its official name is the People's Republic of China. In 1949, after a bitter civil war, Communists took the control of China's government away from the Nationalist Party. The Nationalists fled to the island of Formosa, where they set up a rival government.

Cholon (chō′lôn′). A city in South Vietnam, located just southwest of the capital city, Saigon. Cholon is actually a large suburb of Saigon. See **Saigon.** (See map, pages 8 and 9.)

chromite (krō′mīt). A mineral from which chromium is obtained. Chromium is used in making steel and rust-resistant automobile parts.

cinchona (sin kō′nə). The name of several trees that have bitter bark used in making quinine, a medicine for malaria. Also the name of the bark. See **malaria.**

circumference (sər kum′fər əns). The distance around an object or a geometric figure, especially a circle or a sphere.

collective farm. In Communist countries, a large government-controlled farm with many workers. Must produce what government plans call for, and sell a certain part of the harvest to the government at prices set by the government.

Colombo (kə lum′ bō) **Plan.** A program to aid the economic development of countries in South and Southeast Asia. Provides advice and money, trains workers, and carries on research in agriculture and industry. Several Asian nations participate in this program, as well as Australia, New Zealand, Britain, and the United States.

colony. A territory that is controlled by an outside nation.

Commonwealth of Nations. A voluntary association of independent nations and their dependencies, joined with Britain by economic and historical ties. The British crown is a symbol of the Commonwealth.

communism. Commonly, the teachings and actions of the Communist parties in China, the Soviet Union, and other coun-

tries. Members of these parties are called Communists. They believe that Communist governments must be established throughout the world, by force if necessary. Under this form of government, industry, farming, trade, transportation, communication, education, and most other activities are controlled by the government. There is no democracy as we understand it. See **democracy.**

compass rose. A small drawing included on a map to show directions. A compass rose is often used as a decoration. Here are three examples of compass roses:

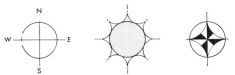

concentration camp. A camp in which people such as political prisoners, prisoners of war, or refugees are confined.

Confucianism (kən fū′shən iz əm). The teachings of Confucius. See **Confucius.**

Confucius (kən fū′shəs) 551?-479 B.C. A Chinese philosopher whose teachings were the main laws of conduct by which China's people lived for more than 2,000 years. Believed that people should show moderation in all actions, obey their elders and rulers, and show a moral sense of responsibility toward their fellowmen.

constitutional monarchy. A country in which the government is headed by a king, queen, or emperor, whose powers are limited by a constitution.

contagious disease. A disease that is spread by contact. The common cold and measles are contagious diseases.

cooperative. A business that is owned by a group of people and is run for their benefit. For example, a group of farmers may form a marketing cooperative to take care of selling their crops.

copra (kop′rə). Dried coconut meat.

Corregidor (kə reg′ə dôr). An island located in the entrance to Manila Bay, in the Philippines. (See map, page 133.) In the early part of World War II, Americans and Filipinos fought bravely here

---

PRONUNCIATION KEY: hat, āge, cãre, fär; let, ēqual, tėrm; it, īce; hot, ōpen, ôrder; oil, out; cup, pùt, rüle, ūse; child; long; thin; ᴛʜen; zh, measure; ə represents a in about, e in taken, i in pencil, o in lemon, u in circus. For the complete key, see page 143.

against overwhelming numbers of Japanese invaders, but were forced to surrender on May 6, 1942.

corrugated iron. A sheet of iron or steel having regularly spaced ripples in it. It is usually coated with zinc to prevent rust. Used mainly for roofs.

crown colony. A colony whose government is controlled to some extent by the British crown.

December 8, 1941. The date in Manila at the time Pearl Harbor, in Hawaii, was being bombed (December 7, 1941). This difference in dates exists because Manila and Pearl Harbor are in different time zones.

degree. A unit of measurement. Any circle may be divided into 360 equal parts, which are called degrees.

delta. A roughly triangular area of land that has been built up of sand and silt deposited at the mouth of a river. The river often splits into branches as it builds up a delta.

democracy. Government by the people. In democratic nations such as the United States, people may form and express their own opinions, choose their leaders, and help decide important issues. In a democracy, government is intended to protect the rights and freedoms of the individual.

diameter (dī am′ə tər). A straight line that goes through the center of a geometric figure, especially a circle or sphere. The line joins two opposite points on the figure.

discrimination. The act of withholding rights or freedoms from people because they belong to a certain group.

Djakarta (jə kär′tə). Formerly called Batavia. Djakarta is the capital and largest city of Indonesia. It is located on the northern coast of western Java. (See map, pages 8 and 9.)

dry rice. Rice that is not raised in flooded fields. It is raised much the same way as wheat.

Dyaks (dī′aks). Brown-skinned people with straight black hair whom the Malays found living in Borneo when they first arrived there. Are divided into several different tribes.

Eastern Hemisphere. The part of the earth in which Europe, Asia, Africa, and Australia are located.

equator (i kwā′tər). An imaginary line around the earth, dividing it into a northern half and a southern half.

Eurasia (yůr ā′zhə). The largest continent on the earth. Some people consider Eurasia to be two separate continents—Europe and Asia.

Eurasian (yůr ā′zhən). A person who is of mixed Asiatic and European descent.

Far East. The eastern part of Asia.

Filipino (fil′ ə pē′ nō). A citizen of the Philippines.

Ford Foundation. An organization established by Henry Ford, founder of Ford Motor Company, and his son, Edsel. Seeks to strengthen peace and democracy, and to improve the lives of men. Makes grants of money to other non-profit organizations, and carries on programs of its own.

French Indochina. The part of Southeast Asia formerly controlled by the French. Cambodia, Laos, and North and South Vietnam now occupy this territory.

Gama (gä′mə), **Vasco da,** 1469?-1524. A Portuguese navigator, who made the first voyage from Europe to India by sailing around the southern tip of Africa (1497-1498).

George Town. Port city located on an island off the northwestern coast of Malaya. Usually called Penang, which is also the name of the island.

great circle. Any imaginary circle around the earth that divides its surface exactly in half. The equator, for example, is a great circle. The shortest route between any two points on the earth always lies on a great circle.

guerrilla (gə ril′ə). Refers mainly to small bands of fighters who usually do not carry much equipment, and who dress as the local people do. They make surprise attacks.

Haiphong (hī′ fông′). A port city in the Red River Delta of North Vietnam. (See map, page 65.)

handicraft. Skilled work, such as weaving or pottery making, that is done by hand.

Hanoi (hä noi′). Capital and largest city of North Vietnam. (See map, page 65.)

Hindu (hin′dü). Refers to the religion of Hinduism. See **Hinduism**. A person who follows this religion.

Hinduism (hin′dü iz əm). The main religion of India and several other parts of Asia. Its followers are called Hindus. They are divided into many groups, or sects, which have different religious customs and worship different gods. Some Hindus believe that these gods are only different forms of the one true spirit of the universe, or God.

Hoa Hao (hō′ə hou′). A religious group in South Vietnam that follows a revised form of Buddhism.

Ho Chi Minh (hō′chē′min′), 1890-1969. President of North Vietnam from 1954 until his death. Ho Chi Minh was born in a village in central Vietnam. When he was in his early twenties, he went to Europe. He became active in politics in France, and in 1920 helped found the French Communist Party. Later he studied in the Soviet Union. In 1925, Ho formed a revolutionary organization that later became the Indochinese Communist Party. From that time onward, he led the Vietnamese in their struggle to gain their independence from France. He formed the Vietnamese Independence League, or Vietminh, in 1941. In 1954, after a bitter war, France gave the Vietminh control over the northern part of Vietnam. However, Ho Chi Minh wanted all of Vietnam to be united under a single government. He worked toward this goal until his death.

hydroelectricity (hī′drō i lek′tris′ə tē). Electricity produced by waterpower. The force of rushing water is used to run machines called generators, which produce electricity.

Indian Ocean. A body of water that lies south of Asia, between Africa and Australia. (See map, pages vi and vii.)

Indo-Chinese Peninsula. A large peninsula extending off the southeastern part of the continent of Asia. (See map, page 2.)

Indonesia (in′dō nē′zhə). The name of the large island group in the southern part of Southeast Asia. Also the name of the independent country that occupies most of this group of islands. (Compare map on page 2 with map on pages 8 and 9.)

Inland Water Transport Board. A government-owned organization in Burma that owns and operates barges, launches, tugs, and paddle-wheel steamers. It was formerly a private company.

Ipoh (ē′pō). A city in northwestern Malaya. (See map, page 130.)

Irrawaddy (ir′ə wod′ē) **River.** The main river of Burma. Begins in the northern part of the country and flows about 1,350 miles southward to the Bay of Bengal. (See map, page 124.)

irrigation. The process of supplying land with water by ditches, canals, sprinklers, pipelines, or other means.

Islam (is′ləm). The religion founded by a prophet named Mohammed, who was born in Arabia in A.D. 570. According to this religion there is only one God, and Mohammed is his prophet. Followers of Islam are called Moslems.

jade. A hard stone that comes in green, white, and other colors. Can be highly polished, and is used to make carved dishes, small statues, and jewelry.

Java (jä′və). The most densely populated island in Indonesia. (See map, pages 8 and 9.)

Jogjakarta (jäg′yə kärt′ə). A city on the island of Java, in Indonesia. (See map, page 65.)

junk. One of several kinds of wooden sailing vessels. Commonly used in China, but now used as far south as Singapore.

jute. A long, glossy fiber used to make burlap bags, twine, and other products. It is obtained from two kinds of tropical plants also known as jute.

Kalimantan (kä′lē män′tän). The Indonesian name for the part of Borneo that is included in the country of Indonesia. (See map, pages 8 and 9.)

PRONUNCIATION KEY: hat, āge, cãre, fär; let, ēqual, tèrm; it, īce; hot, ōpen, ôrder; oil, out; cup, pùt, rüle, ūse; child; long, thin; ᴛHen; zh, measure; ə represents a in about, e in taken, i in pencil, o in lemon, u in circus. For the complete key, see page 143.

kapok (kā′pok). The silky fibers that grow around the seeds of the kapok tree. Because kapok is highly moistureproof, it is often used in making life preservers and as insulation.

Karen (kə ren′). A group of tribes in Burma and the part of Thailand near the Burmese border. Live mainly in the highlands, but some also live in the delta of the Irrawaddy.

Khmers (kmerz). Refers to a group of people from whom most present-day Cambodians are descended. In the sixth century, the Khmers began to conquer their neighbors. They established a great empire with its capital at Angkor. See **Angkor**.

Kuala Lumpur (kwä′lə lùm′pür′). Largest city and capital of Malaysia. (See map, page 65.)

Kuching (kü′ching). Largest city of Sarawak, a state of Malaysia, located on the island of Borneo. (See map, page 131.)

lacquer (lak′ər) **ware.** Articles, such as trays and boxes, that have been coated with a special type of varnish.

land reform laws. Laws passed to improve the economic and social conditions of farmers. These laws aim to help farmers rent land at reasonable rates or obtain farms of their own.

Lao (lä′ō). Refers to the largest group of people in Laos. Also, refers to their language. See **Laos**.

Laos (lä′ōs). A country in the eastern part of the Indo-Chinese Peninsula. (Compare map on page 2 with map on pages 8 and 9.)

latitude. Distance north or south of the equator, measured in degrees. (See Skills Manual, page 6.)

Legaspi. See **López de Legaspi.**

Lesser Sunda (sun′də) **Islands.** A chain of islands in the archipelago of Indonesia. Bali is the westernmost island in this chain, and Timor is the easternmost. (See map, pages 8 and 9.)

Leyte (lā′tē). One of the eleven main islands in the Philippines. (See map, page 133.)

Lombok (lom bok′). A small island in Indonesia. Located east of Bali. (See map, pages 8 and 9.)

López de Legaspi (lō′pās ŦHä lä gäs′pē), **Miguel,** 1510?-1572. A Spanish soldier who succeeded in establishing the first permanent Spanish settlement in the Philippines.

Luzon (lü zon′). The main island in the Philippines. (See map, page 133.)

Magellan (mə jel′ən), **Ferdinand,** 1480?-1521. Son of a Portuguese nobleman. Served as a soldier and sailor for Portugal. Was accused of trading with the enemy, and lost the friendship of the King. Gave up his Portuguese citizenship, and offered to find a westward route to the Moluccas, or Spice Islands, for Spain. Sailed as far as the Philippines, where he was killed. One of his ships completed the first voyage around the world.

Malacca (mə lak′ə). A port city on the southwestern coast of Malaya. (See map, page 35.) Was formerly the most important trading city in Southeast Asia.

Malacca, Strait of. Narrow sea passage between Malaya and Sumatra, connecting the South China Sea with the Indian Ocean. (See map, pages 8 and 9.)

malaria (mə lär′ē ə). A disease that is carried from person to person by a certain kind of mosquito. Destroys blood cells and causes chills and fever.

Malaya (mə lā′ə). Common name for the eleven Malayan states, which occupy the southern part of the Malay Peninsula. Part of Malaysia. See **Malaysia**.

Malay (mā′lā) **Peninsula.** The long, narrow body of land that extends southward from the Indo-Chinese Peninsula. (See map, page 2.)

Malaysia (mə lā′zhə). A nation in Southeast Asia, formed in 1963. Includes the eleven Malayan states, Sarawak, and Sabah. (See map, pages 8 and 9.)

Maluku (mə lü′kü). A group of islands in eastern Indonesia. Also called the Moluccas or the Spice Islands. (See map, pages 8 and 9.)

Manchuria (man chùr′ē ə). The name given by Americans and Europeans to the northeastern part of China.

manganese (mang′gə nēs). A grayish white metal. Often used with other metals to make them harder and tougher.

mango. The name of a tropical fruit with juicy orange or yellow pulp, a large seed, and leathery skin. Usually about the size and shape of a pear. Also the name of the tree on which this fruit grows.

Manila (mə nil′ə). The largest city and main port of the Philippines. Located on the island of Luzon. (See map, page 65.)

marsupials (mär sü′pē əlz). The group of animals that includes the kangaroo and the opossum. A female marsupial carries her young in a pouch at the front of her body.

Masbate (mäs bä′tä). One of the eleven main islands in the Philippines. (See map, page 133.)

Mekong (mā′kong′) **River.** A river about 2,600 miles long. Begins in Tibet and flows through southern China and the eastern part of the Indo-Chinese Peninsula to the South China Sea.

Mercator (mėr kā′tər) **projection.** One of many possible arrangements of meridians and parallels on which a map of the world may be drawn. It was devised by Gerhardus Mercator, a Flemish geographer who lived from 1512 to 1594. On a Mercator map, all meridians are drawn straight up and down, with north at the top. The parallels are drawn straight across, but increasingly farther apart toward the poles. If you will compare the first section, or gore, of the "orange-peel" map on page 7 of the Skills Manual with the section of the Mercator map directly below it, you will see how the Mercator map straightens out the meridians. Because the earth features have been stretched in an east-west direction, except at the equator, they appear wider in the Mercator section than they do in the "orange-peel" section. To make up for this east-west stretching, earth features on the Mercator map are also stretched in a north-south direction. Therefore, on Mercator maps the shapes of landmasses and bodies of water are fairly accurate, but their sizes are not.

millet (mil′it). One of several kinds of grass that produce clusters of grain. It is raised for its grain and for hay.

Mindanao (min′də nä′ō). The second largest island in the Philippines. (See map, page 133.)

Mindoro (min dô′rō). One of the eleven main islands in the Philippines. (See map, page 133.)

Mogul (mō′gul). Refers to people of the Mongolian race, especially the 16th century conquerors of India or their descendants.

Mohammed (mō ham′id), A.D. 570-632. A prophet and the founder of Islam, the religion of the Moslems. See **Islam**.

Moluccas (mə luk′əz). See **Maluku**.

molybdenum (mə lib′də nəm). A silvery-white metal that melts at a very high temperature. Used to strengthen and harden steel.

Mongols (mong′glz). People from Mongolia, in east central Asia. In the thirteenth century, Mongol armies overran China and other parts of Asia, as well as parts of Europe.

Moorish architecture. The style of building developed by the Moslems from northern Africa who invaded Spain. Uses arches and slender pillars.

Moros (mô′rōz). Moslem Filipinos on the island of Mindanao and in the Sulu Archipelago of the Philippines.

Moslem (moz′ləm). Refers to the religion of Islam or to one of its followers. See **Islam**.

mosque (mosk). A Moslem temple of worship. See **Moslem**.

Moulmein (mül mān′). A port city in Burma. (See map, page 65.)

Negros (nā′grōs). One of the eleven main islands in the Philippines. (See map, page 133.)

neutral. A person, group, or country that does not take sides in a quarrel or war.

nickel. A silvery-white metal that is very hard. Is used in mixtures of metals and for plating articles made of other metals.

PRONUNCIATION KEY: hat, āge, cāre, fär; let, ēqual, tėrm; it, īce; hot, ōpen, ôrder; oil, out; cup, pùt, rüle, ūse; child; long; thin; ͬＨen; zh, measure; ə represents a in about, e in taken, i in pencil, o in lemon, u in circus. For the complete key, see page 143.

nipa (nē′pə). A type of palm that grows in Southeast Asia.

Norodom Sihanouk (nôr′ä dəm sē′hä nůk), 1922- . Chief of state of Cambodia from 1960 to 1970. Was formerly the country's king, but gave up the throne in 1955.

North Borneo. A former British colony on the island of Borneo. Now called Sabah. See **Sabah**.

North Vietnam. See **Vietnam**.

oil palm. Any one of a group of palms. Its fruit is about the size of a date and grows in bunches. Both the flesh and the seeds of this fruit provide oil.

opium (ō′pē əm). A habit-forming drug made from the juice of a certain kind of poppy. Used in making several medicines that relieve pain.

Pagan (pə gän′). A ruined city in Burma. Formerly the capital of a powerful Burmese kingdom. (See map, page 65.)

pagoda (pə gō′də). A towerlike structure. It is usually a memorial or a temple.

Palawan (pä lä′wän). One of the eleven main islands in the Philippines. (See map, page 133.)

palm sugar. Sugar made from the sap of certain types of palm trees.

Panay (pä nī′). One of the eleven main islands in the Philippines. (See map, page 133.)

pandan (pan′dən) leaves. The leaves of plants belonging to the pandanus, or screw-pine, family. Shrubs or trees belonging to this plant group have one main stem and a few branches with tufts of narrow leaves at the ends.

papaya (pə pä′yə). A melonlike tropical fruit that varies from orange to yellow in color. Grows on the papaya tree, which looks somewhat like a palm.

parallel. One of the imaginary lines that encircles the earth parallel to the equator. Used to help locate places on the earth.

parliament (pär′lə mənt). The lawmaking branch of a country's government.

Pearl Harbor. An inlet on the southern coast of Oahu, the main island of Hawaii. A United States naval base is located here.

Penang (pi nang′). Leading seaport and second largest city of Malaysia. Located on an island, also called Penang, off the northwestern coast of Malaya. The city of Penang is also called George Town. (See map, page 65.)

per capita income. The total income of all of the people in a country divided by the number of people. Per capita figures are often rough guesses, for it is difficult to obtain correct figures.

Philippine mahogany. Any of several different trees in the Philippines, the wood of which is somewhat like mahogany.

Philippines (fil′ə pēnz). An island country located southeast of the continent of Asia. (See map, pages 8 and 9.)

Phnom Penh (pə nom′ pen′). The capital and largest city of Cambodia. (See map, page 65.)

phosphate (fos′fāt). A mineral substance found in certain rocks and in other sources. Phosphate is used in making fertilizers.

Ping River. A river in western Thailand. Begins above Chiang Mai and flows about 360 miles southeastward to join with another river to form the Chao Phraya. See **Chao Phraya**.

plateau. A large, generally level area of high land.

pope. Head of the Roman Catholic Church.

Portuguese (pôr′chə gēz′). People from Portugal, a country in southwestern Europe.

Portuguese Timor. An Overseas Province of Portugal that occupies the eastern part of the island of Timor and some small nearby islands. Timor is the largest of the Lesser Sunda Islands, in the archipelago of Indonesia. (See map on pages 8 and 9.) Portuguese Timor covers an area of 5,763 square miles and has a population of about 590,000. Among the crops raised here are corn, rice, copra, and rubber.

premier. In many countries, the government official who heads the cabinet.

prime minister. Another name for premier. See **premier**.

protectorate. A nation that is controlled by a stronger nation. The stronger nation protects and helps to govern the weaker one.

proteins (prō'tēnz). A group of substances found in the cells of plants and animals. Living things must have proteins in order to repair damaged cells and build new ones. Good food sources of proteins are eggs, meat, and soybeans.

pulses. A group of plants that includes peas and beans. Also, the edible seeds of these plants.

Quezon (kā'sôn) **City.** The capital of the Philippines. Located on the island of Luzon. (See map, page 65.)

quinine (kwī'nīn). See cinchona.

radiotelephone. A telephone that uses radio waves instead of connecting wires.

Raffles, Sir Stamford, 1781-1826. A British colonial official. Founded Singapore to prevent Holland from gaining control of trade in Southeast Asia.

rainforest. Commonly, a dense forest found in tropical areas that have no dry season and receive very heavy rainfall. A rainforest consists mostly of tall, broad-leaved evergreen trees.

Ramayana (rä mä'yə nə). One of the two great story-poems of India. It tells of the adventures of a brave and noble prince named Rama, who was really a god in human form.

Rangoon (rang gün'). Capital and largest city of Burma. (See map, page 65.)

rattan (ra tan'). Any palm that has a long, climbing stem. Provides a tough material, also called rattan, used in making furniture and other articles.

republic (ri pub'lik). A nation having a form of government in which power rests with its citizens. The people govern themselves indirectly through the officers and representatives whom they elect to carry on the work of government.

Sabah (sä'bə). A state of Malaysia. Formerly, a British colony called North Borneo. (See map, pages 8 and 9.)

sago (sā'gō). A starch prepared from the spongy center of several types of tropical palm trees. The tree is cut down, and the center is removed, ground, washed, and strained. After more washings, a flour is produced that is used in making puddings and soups, and as a stiffening for textiles.

Saigon (sī gon'). Capital of South Vietnam. Saigon and its large suburb Cholon together form the largest urban area in the country. (See map, page 65.)

Sarawak (sə rä'wäk). A state of Malaysia. Formerly, a British colony on the island of Borneo. (See map, pages 8 and 9.)

Savang Vatthana (sə wäng' wat'tə nä), 1907- . King of Laos. Came to the throne in 1959.

SEATO. Short name for Southeast Asia Treaty Organization. Members are the United States, the United Kingdom, France, Australia, New Zealand, Pakistan, Thailand, and the Philippines. Was formed for the purpose of preserving peace in Southeast Asia and the Southwest Pacific by helping the member nations of this area defend themselves against military aggression. The United States joined with the understanding that this meant Communist aggression only.

sesamum. An herb that produces small, flattish seeds. These are used for their oil, and as a food. Also called sesame.

Shwe Dagon (shwä' dä gôn') **Pagoda.** A large Buddhist temple in Rangoon, Burma. (See picture, pages 66 and 67.)

Siam (sī am'). The former name of Thailand. See **Thailand.**

Siam, Gulf of. An arm of the South China Sea, bordered by Thailand, Cambodia, and South Vietnam. (See map, pages 8 and 9.)

Sihanouk. See **Norodom Sihanouk.**

silt. A muddy material that is finer than sand but not so fine as clay.

Singapore. An island country off the Malay Peninsula. Also the name of the port city on the island. (See map, page 136.)

sisal (sis'l). A strong, long-lasting fiber used in making different kinds of twine.

sorghum (sôr'gəm). The name given to a group of tall, canelike plants of the grass family. Some types of sorghum provide

PRONUNCIATION KEY: hat, āge, cãre, fär; let, ēqual, tėrm; it, īce; hot, ōpen, ôrder; oil, out; cup, pùt, rüle, ūse; child; long; thin; ŦHen; zh, measure; ə represents a in about, e in taken, i in pencil, o in lemon, u in circus. For the complete key, see page 143.

151

a sweet juice for making syrup, and others provide grain. Sorghum is also used for animal feed.

South Vietnam. See **Vietnam.**

Souvanna Phouma (sü wän′ä pü′mä), 1900- A prince of one branch of the royal family in Laos. He has been the country's premier since 1962.

Spice Islands. See **Maluku.**

square inch. A unit for measuring area, equal to the area of a square that measures one inch on each side.

standard of living. The average level of conditions in a community or country, or the level of conditions people consider necessary for a happy, satisfying life. In countries with a high standard of living, many different goods and services are considered to be necessities. In countries with a low standard of living, many of these same items are luxuries enjoyed by only a few people.

strait. A narrow passage of water connecting two large bodies of water.

Suharto (sü här′tō), 1921- . An army general who became president of Indonesia in 1968. Son of a Moslem merchant in Java. During the 1940's, Suharto served with military forces fighting for Indonesia's independence. Later he became deputy chief of staff of the Indonesian army. In 1967, Suharto was named acting president of Indonesia when President Sukarno was removed from office.

Sukarno (sü kär′nō), 1901-1970. First president of Indonesia. Son of a schoolteacher in Java. After receiving a degree in engineering, Sukarno became active in the movement for independence. Was imprisoned and later exiled by the Dutch. During World War II, continued to work for independence. After Japan surrendered, he declared Indonesia to be independent and was chosen the first president. See **Suharto.**

Sulawesi (sü′lä wä′sē). A large island in Indonesia. Formerly called Celebes. (See map, pages 8 and 9.)

sultan (sult′n). The ruler of a Moslem state.

sultanate (sult′n āt). The territory governed by a sultan. See **sultan.**

Sultan of Sulu. See **sultan** and **Sulu Archipelago.**

Sulu (sü′lü) **Archipelago.** A chain of small islands in the southwestern part of the Philippines. (See map, page 133.) Inhabited largely by Moros. In about the fifteenth century was united under a sultan. In 1940, the Sultan ceded the archipelago to the Philippines. See **Moros, sultan, sultanate.**

Sumatra (sü mä′trə). Second most important island in Indonesia. (See map, pages 8 and 9.)

Surabaja (sü′rä bä′yä). A port city in eastern Java. (See map, page 65.)

Tagalog (tä gä′log). The language of one of the largest groups of people in the Philippines. Tagalog, English, and Spanish are the three main languages of the country.

Tamil (tam′l). The language of a group of people in southern India. Also the name of these people. Many Tamils now live in Southeast Asia.

Taoism (tou′iz əm). A philosophy and religion, traditionally founded by a Chinese thinker named Lao-tzu, born about 604 B.C. He taught that there was only one true principle for people to follow. This was the *Tao,* which might be called "The Way." Nature had its beginning in the *Tao* and followed its law. To find happiness, men had to give up pride and ambition, and live simply, as creatures in the world of nature did. Today, spirit worship and magic ceremonies have become an important part of Taoism.

Tenasserim (tə nas′ər im). The part of Burma that extends into the Malay Peninsula. (See map, page 124.)

terraced. Refers to strips of level farmland that have been made on hillsides. (See picture, pages 82 and 83.)

Thai (tī). Refers to Thailand and its largest group of people. Also, refers to a group of people from whom the present-day Thai, the Lao, and a group of tribesmen called the Shan are descended. See **Lao.**

Thailand (tī′land). A country in Southeast Asia, located on the Indo-Chinese and the Malay peninsulas. (Compare map on page 2 with map on pages 8 and 9.)

three-dimensional (də men'shən l). Having height, width, and length.

Timor (tē'môr). An island in the archipelago of Indonesia. Indonesia governs part of the island. The rest is governed by Portugal. See **Indonesia** and **Portuguese Timor**.

Tjiliwong (chē'lē wông) **River**. A river about 50 miles long. Located in the western part of Java, in Indonesia.

topographic (top'ə graf'ik). Refers to the physical features of an area, such as lakes, rivers, and hills. A topographic map shows the elevation of these features and their location in relation to each other.

tuberculosis. An infectious disease that wastes away tissues and causes small, rounded growths, often in the lungs.

tungsten (tung'stən). A grayish white metal. Used in making high-quality steel, wires for electric light bulbs, and other products.

underdeveloped. Refers to those countries in which most work is done by the muscle power of men and animals. In underdeveloped countries, many natural resources are poorly used and the standard of living is low. In contrast are the developed countries, in which most work is done by power-driven machinery, resources are used extensively, and the general standard of living is high.

UNESCO. Short name for United Nations Educational, Scientific, and Cultural Organization. An agency of the United Nations. See **United Nations**.

United Kingdom. Short name for the United Kingdom of Great Britain and Northern Ireland. Also popularly known as Britain or Great Britain.

United Nations. An organization formed in 1945 to work for world peace. More than 130 nations are members. Agencies related to the United Nations work to solve problems in fields such as health, agriculture, and labor.

veneer (və nir'). A thin sheet of wood. Is usually cut from a log of good quality, then glued onto a piece of cheaper wood.

Vientiane (vyen'tyän'). The largest city and administrative capital of Laos. (See map, page 126.)

Vietnam (vē et'näm'). A part of French Indochina that was divided into two countries in 1954. (See **French Indochina**.) These two countries, North Vietnam and South Vietnam, are in the eastern part of the Indo-Chinese Peninsula. (Compare map on page 2 with map on pages 8 and 9.)

Visayas (vi sä'yəz). A large group of islands in the central part of the Philippines. (See map, pages 8 and 9.)

Western. In this book, refers to Europe and to the United States and other countries whose civilization developed from that of Europe.

Westerners. People of the Western nations. See **Western**.

West Irian (ir'ē än'). The western part of the island of New Guinea. (See map, pages 8 and 9.) West Irian belongs to Indonesia.

World Bank. Short name commonly used for the International Bank for Reconstruction and Development. It has its headquarters in Washington, D.C. The governments of more than 115 countries are members of this bank and contribute money to it. When these nations need money for building highways, constructing dams, or making other improvements, they may borrow it from the World Bank.

World War II, 1939-1945. The second war in history that involved nearly every part of the world. The Allies, which included China, the United States, the United Kingdom, the Soviet Union, and many other countries, defeated the Axis. The Axis included mainly Germany, Italy, and Japan. The Soviet Union, the United States, and Japan did not enter the war until 1941.

yaws. A tropical disease that causes sores on the skin. Very contagious.

INDEX

Explanation of abbreviations used in this Index:

p — picture   *m* — map

PRONUNCIATION KEY: hat, āge, câre, fär; let, ēqual, tèrm; it, īce; hot, ōpen, ôrder; oil, out; cup, pùt, rüle, ūse; child; long; thin; ŦHen; zh, measure; ə represents a in about, e in taken, i in pencil, o in lemon, u in circus. For the complete key, see page 143.

PRONUNCIATION KEY: hat, āge, cāre, fär; let, ēqual, tèrm; it, īce; hot, ōpen, ôrder; oil, out; cup, pùt, rüle, ūse; child; long; thin; ŧHen; zh, measure; ə represents a in about, e in taken, i in pencil, o in lemon, u in circus. For the complete key, see page 143.

Maps, Charts, and Special Features

Acknowledgments

Grateful acknowledgment is made to the following for permission to use the illustrations found in this book:

Alfred T. Palmer: Pages 4-5
Alpha Photo Associates, Inc.: Page 120; page 60 by Wagg
Authenticated News International: Pages 46 and 48
Carl E. Östman: Single edition pages x-xi by Ralp Herrmans
Design Photographers International, Inc.: Single edition pages xii-xiii
Eastfoto: Single edition page xvi
Embassy of South Vietnam: Pages 61 and 104-105
Embassy of the Federation of Malaya: Page 33
Freelance Photographers Guild: Page 69; pages 2-3 by Hanes
Ginn and Company: Page 37
H. Armstrong Roberts: Pages 90-91 and 105
Harrison Forman: Pages 28-29 and 94-95
J. Allan Cash: Pages 114-115
KLM Royal Dutch Airlines: Page 134
Magnum Photos, Inc.: Page 118; pages 116-117 by Marc Riboud; pages 122-123 by Philip Jones Griffiths
National Palace Museum: Pages 32-33
Paul Almasy: Pages 12, 16-17, 38-39, and 88. Single edition pages iv-v
Peter Hickman: Pages 72-73

Photo Researchers, Inc.: Pages 44-45; pages 10-11, 22-23, 62-63, and 73 by Jules Bucher; pages 14-15 by Jack Fields; pages 18-19 by V. Englebert; page 24 by John Lewis Stage; pages 30-31, 58-59, 68, 106-107, 109, and 137 by Van Bucher; page 31 by George Holton; page 43 by Jerry Cooke; pages 55 and 110-111 by Miriam Bucher; pages 66-67 by Stephanie Dinkins; pages 70-71 by Susan Mc Cartney; pages 80-81 and 81 by Helen and Frank Schreider; pages 108-109 by Frank Schreider; page 136 by Ewing Kranin. Single edition pages xiv-xv by Van Bucher
Rapho Guillumette Pictures: Pages 20-21 by Inger Mc Cabe; page 34 by Brian Brake; pages 64 and 102-103 by Georg Gerster. Single edition page viii
R. Bunnag: Pages 112-113
Shostal Associates, Inc.: Pages 6-7, 26-27, 50-51, 74-75, 78-79, 86-87, 88-89, 98-99, and 140; pages 82-83 and 92 by D. J. Forbert. Single edition pages ii-iii
Three Lions, Inc.: Pages 56-57 and 132; page 139 by Horace Bristol
United Nations: Pages 52-53, 76, 84, 96-97, 100-101, and 138
United States Army: Pages 40-41

Grateful acknowledgment is made to Scott, Foresman and Company for the pronunciation system used in this book, which is taken from the Thorndike-Barnhart Dictionary Series.
Grateful acknowledgment is made to the following for permission to use cartographic data in this book: Creative Arts: Globes on page 19, and top maps on page 10 of the Skills Manual; Nystrom Raised Relief Map Company, Chicago 60618: Page ix, and bottom map on page 10 of the Skills Manual; Panoramic Studios: Page vi; Rand McNally & Company: Pages vi-vii and pages 1 and 6; United States Department of Commerce, Bureau of the Census: Top map on page 9 of the Skills Manual.

SKILLS MANUAL

CONTENTS

Thinking and Solving Problems

Why the social studies are important to you. During the next few years, you will make an important choice. You will choose whether or not you will direct your own life. Many people are never aware of making this choice. They drift through life, never really trying to understand what is going on around them or why things turn out the way they do. Without knowing it, these people have chosen not to direct their own lives. As a result, they miss many enriching experiences. Other people make a serious effort to choose a way of life that will bring them satisfaction. If you decide to live by choice instead of by chance, you will be able to live a more satisfying life.

You will need three types of knowledge to live by choice successfully. Living by choice will demand a great deal from you. You will have to keep growing in three different types of learnings — understandings, values and attitudes, and skills. As the chart on the next page shows, the type of learnings we call understandings includes the kinds of information you need in order to understand yourself, your country, and your world. The type of learnings we call values and attitudes deals with the way you feel toward yourself and your world. The third type of learnings includes the skills you need to use in gaining understandings and developing constructive values and attitudes. Among these skills are those you need for obtaining and using knowledge, and for working effectively with other people.

The social studies can help you grow in the three types of learnings. Your social studies class is one of the best places in which you can explore the three types of learnings. Here you can obtain much of the information you need for understanding yourself and your world. You can practice many important skills. Through many experiences, you can begin to evaluate what in life is worthwhile to you.

The problem-solving method will help you achieve success in social studies. Since the social studies are of such great importance, you want to use the best possible study method. You could just read a textbook and memorize answers for a test. If you did so, however, you would forget much of the information soon after the test was over. Your thinking ability would not improve, and you would not gain new, constructive values and attitudes. You would not have the opportunity to use many important skills, either. We suggest that you use a special way of studying called the problem-solving method. You will want to use the problem-solving method as you do research in this book. To use this method, follow these steps.

1. Do some general background reading about a topic such as land, people, natural resources, or industry.

2. Choose an important, interesting problem that you would like to solve. Write it down so that you will have clearly in mind what it is you want to find out. (Look at the sample problem on page 4.) If there are small problems that need to be solved in order to solve your big problem, list them, too.

3. Consider all possible solutions to your problem and list the ones that seem most likely to be true. These possible solutions are called "educated guesses," or hypotheses. You will try to solve your problem by finding facts to support or disprove your hypotheses.

4. Test your hypotheses by doing research. This book provides you with four main sources of information. These are the pictures, the text, the maps, and the Glossary. To locate the information you need, you may use the Table of Contents

Thinking and the Three Types of Learnings

THINKING

One of the main reasons you are attending school is to develop your ability to think clearly. Thinking includes seven different thought processes. (See definitions below.) If you learn to use your higher thought processes, rather than simply repeat information you have memorized, you will achieve greater success in school and in life. In fact, your ability to fulfill your obligations as a citizen will depend largely on how well you learn to think. Your ability to think clearly will also help you make progress in the three types of learnings included in the social studies. (See chart below.)

Seven Thought Processes

1. **Remembering** is recalling or recognizing information.
2. **Translation** is changing information from one form into another, such as words into pictures.
3. **Interpretation** is discovering relationships among facts, concepts,* and generalizations.*
4. **Application** is applying the appropriate knowledge and skills to the solution of a new problem.
5. **Analysis** is separating complicated material into its basic parts to see how those parts were put together, how they are related to each other, and how the parts are related to the whole.
6. **Synthesis** is putting ideas together in a form that is not only meaningful but also new and original.
7. **Evaluation** is judging whether something is acceptable or unacceptable, according to definite standards.

THREE TYPES OF LEARNINGS

Understandings	Values and Attitudes	Skills
Concepts	Beliefs	Obtaining knowledge
Generalizations	Appreciations	Using knowledge
Facts	Ideas	Working with others

Understandings
You will truly gain an understanding of important concepts and generalizations when you use your thought processes to organize information in meaningful ways. In turn, the concepts and generalizations you develop will help you learn to think critically about new situations you meet.

Values and Attitudes
You will develop many constructive values and attitudes as you improve your thinking ability. Success in the higher levels of thinking will bring you faith that you can solve problems and make wise decisions. In turn, positive values and attitudes will help you to develop your thinking ability.

Skills
You will be more successful in developing the social studies skills when you use your higher thought processes described above. In turn, you will find that the social studies skills will help you do the critical thinking needed for solving the many difficult problems you will face during your lifetime.

*See Four Words To Understand, page 4

and the Index. The suggestions on pages 12-15 will help you to locate and evaluate other sources of information.

As you do research, make notes of all the information you find that will either support your hypotheses or disprove them. You may discover that information from one source disagrees with information from another. If this should happen, check still further and try to decide which facts are correct.

5. **Summarize what you have learned.** Have you been able to support one or more of your hypotheses with facts? Have you been able to disprove one or more of your hypotheses? What new facts have you learned? Do you need to do further research?

You may want to write a report about the problem. To help other people share the ideas that you have come to understand, you may decide to illustrate your research project with maps, pictures, or your own drawings. You will find helpful suggestions for writing a good report on pages 15-17.

You can use the problem-solving method throughout your life. In addition to helping you to achieve success in the social studies, the problem-solving method can help you in another way. By using it, you will learn to deal with problems in a way that will be valuable to you throughout your life. Many successful scientists, businessmen, and government leaders use this method to solve problems.

A sample problem to solve. As you study this book, you may wish to solve the following sample problem.

Since World War II, Southeast Asia has been one of the world's most troubled areas. Why has there been so much unrest in this region? In forming hypotheses, you will need to consider facts about:

1. the history of Southeast Asia before World War II
2. the standard of living in this region
3. the governments of the countries in Southeast Asia
4. Communist intervention in Southeast Asia

Four Words To Understand

1. **A concept** is a big, general idea that includes many smaller, more specific ideas. An example of a concept is the idea of "trade." Many kinds of exchange are included in this idea. Two boys who exchange marbles on the playground are carrying on trade. A woman who pays money to the grocer for a loaf of bread is also carrying on trade; so is a factory that buys raw materials from other countries and sells its manufactured products overseas. Only as you come to see the various things that the word "trade" includes do you grow to understand this concept. Another example of a concept is the idea of "climate."

2. **A generalization** is a general rule or principle that expresses a meaningful relationship among two or more concepts. It is formed by drawing a conclusion from a group of facts. For example, "Through trade, all people on the earth can have a better living," is a generalization drawn from facts about trade and the way people live in various parts of the world. It includes the concepts: "trade," "all people,"

"the earth," and "a better living." These have been put together to give a significant understanding about the world. The many facts you read about, hear about, or experience will make more sense if you think of them as statements that can be combined to form meaningful generalizations. Remember, however, that if a generalization is based on wrong or insufficient facts, or is carelessly thought out, it may be false. Make certain that you understand the concepts in a generalization, and judge carefully whether or not you think it is true.

3. **Values** are the things in life that a person considers right, desirable, or worthwhile. For instance, if you believe that every individual is important, we may say that one of your values is the worth of the individual.

4. **Attitudes** are the outward expression of a person's values. For example, a person who truly values the worth of every individual will express this value by treating everyone he meets with consideration.

Learning Map Skills

The earth is a sphere. Our earth is round like a ball. We call any object with this shape a sphere. The earth is, of course, a very large sphere. Its diameter* is about 8,000 miles. Its circumference* is about 25,000 miles. The earth is not quite a perfect sphere, however, for it is slightly flattened at the North and South poles.

Globes and maps. The globe in your classroom is also a sphere. It is a model of the earth. The surface of the globe shows the shapes of the landmasses and bodies of water on the earth. By looking at the globe, you can see exactly where the continents, islands, and oceans are located. Globes are made with the North Pole at the top, but they are usually tilted to represent the way that the earth is tilted. Maps are flat drawings that represent part or all of the earth's surface.

Scale. Globes and maps give information about distance. When you use them, you need to know how many miles on the earth are represented by a given distance on the globe or map. This relationship is called the scale. The scale of a globe or map may be expressed in several different ways.

On most maps, the scale is shown by a small drawing. For example:

Scale of Miles   0   200   400

Sometimes, the scale is expressed in this way: 1 inch = 400 miles.

Scale is often shown in another way, especially on globes and large maps. For example: 1:10,000,000. These numbers mean that any given distance on the globe or map represents a distance on the earth that is ten million times as large. When the scale is shown in this way, you may use any kind of measuring unit you wish. If you choose the inch, then one inch on the globe or map equals ten million inches on the earth, or about 158 miles. You might, however, prefer to use the centimeter,* another measuring unit. In that case, one centimeter on the globe or map would represent ten million centimeters on the earth, or 100 kilometers.

*See Glossary

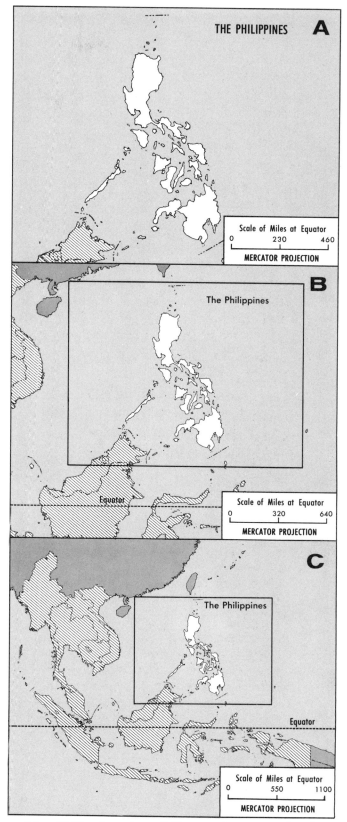

The Philippines is a different size on each of the three maps above. This is because one inch on each of these maps represents a different distance on the surface of the earth.

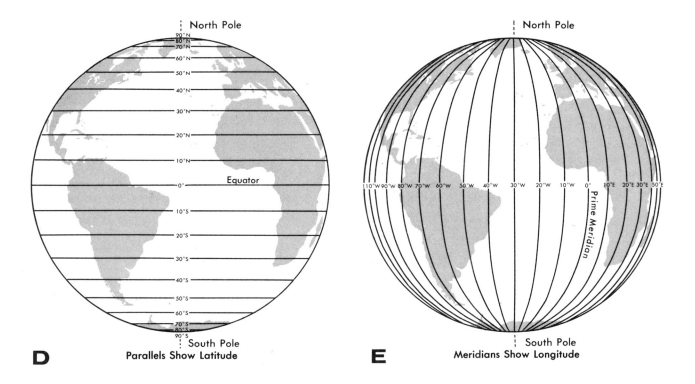

North Pole

90°N
80°N
70°N
60°N
50°N
40°N
30°N
20°N
10°N
0° — Equator
10°S
20°S
30°S
40°S
50°S
60°S
70°S
80°S
90°S

South Pole

D   Parallels Show Latitude

North Pole

110°W 90°W 80°W 70°W 60°W 50°W 40°W 30°W 20°W 10°W 0° 10°E 20°E 30°E 50°E

Prime Meridian

South Pole

E   Meridians Show Longitude

Locating places on the earth. Map makers, travelers, and other curious people have always wanted to know just where certain places are located. Over the years, a very accurate way of giving such information has been worked out. This system is used all over the world.

In order to work out a system for locating anything, you need starting points and a measuring unit. The North and South poles and the equator are the starting points for the system we use to locate places on the earth. The measuring unit for our system is called the degree (°).

Parallels show latitude. When we want to locate a place on the earth, we first find out how far it is north or south of the equator. This distance measured in degrees is called north or south latitude. The equator represents zero latitude. The North Pole is located at 90 degrees north latitude, and the South Pole is at 90 degrees south latitude.

All points on the earth that have the same latitude are the same distance from the equator. A line connecting such points is called a parallel. This is because it is parallel to the equator. (See illustration D, above.)

Meridians show longitude. After we know the latitude of a place, we need to know its location in an east-west direction. This is called its longitude. The lines that show longitude are called meridians. They are drawn so as to connect the North and South poles. (See illustration E, above.) Longitude is measured from the meridian that passes through Greenwich, England. This line of zero longitude is called the prime meridian. Distance east or west of this meridian measured in degrees is called east or west longitude. The meridian of 180 degrees west longitude is the same as the one of 180 degrees east longitude. This is because 180 degrees is exactly halfway around the world from the prime meridian.

Locating places on a globe. The location of a certain place might be given to you like this: 30°N 90°W. This means that this place is located 30 degrees north of the equator, and 90 degrees west of the prime meridian. See if you can find this place on the globe in your classroom. It is helpful to remember that parallels and meridians are drawn every ten or fifteen degrees on most globes.

The round earth on a flat map. An important fact about a sphere is that you cannot flatten out its surface perfectly. To prove this, you might perform an experiment. Cut an orange in half and scrape away the fruit. You will not be able to press either piece of orange peel flat without crushing it. If you cut one piece in half, however, you can press these smaller pieces nearly flat. Next, cut one of these pieces of peel into three sections, or gores, shaped like those in illustration F, below. You will be able to press these small sections quite flat.

A map like the one shown in illustration F can be made by cutting the surface of a globe into twelve pieces shaped like the smallest sections of your orange peel. Such a map would be fairly accurate. However, an "orange-peel" map is not an easy map to use, because the continents and oceans are split apart.

A flat map can never show the earth's surface as truthfully as a globe can. On globes, shape, size, distance, and direction are all accurate. Although a single flat map of the world cannot be drawn to show all four of these things correctly, flat maps can be made that show some of these things accurately. The various ways of drawing maps of the world to show different things correctly are called map projections.

The Mercator* projection. Illustration G, below, shows a world map called a Mercator projection. When you compare this map

A Round Globe on a Flat Surface

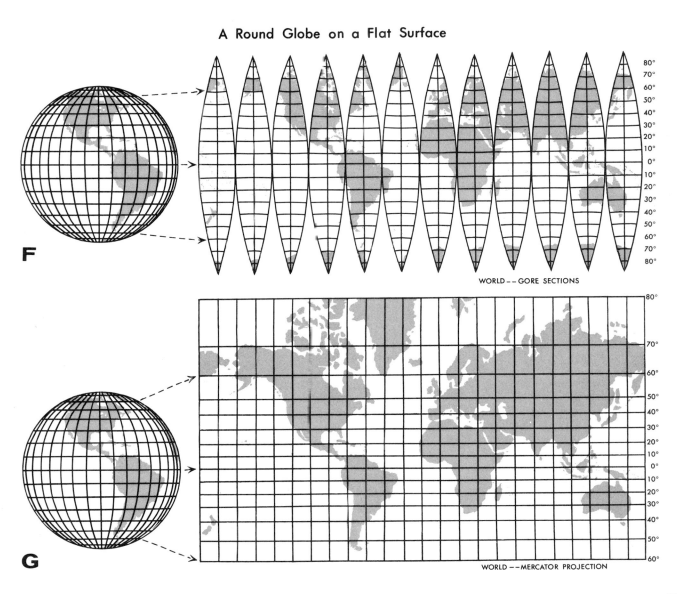

WORLD -- GORE SECTIONS

WORLD -- MERCATOR PROJECTION

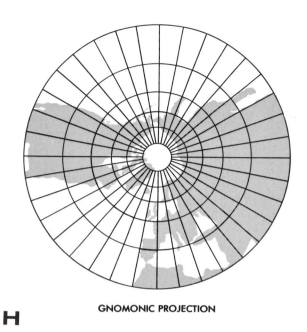

H GNOMONIC PROJECTION

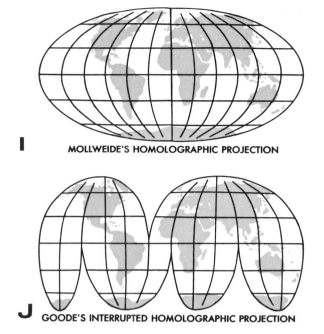

I MOLLWEIDE'S HOMOLOGRAPHIC PROJECTION

J GOODE'S INTERRUPTED HOMOLOGRAPHIC PROJECTION

with a globe, you can see that continents, islands, and oceans have almost the right shape. On this kind of map, however, North America seems larger than Africa, which is not true. On Mercator maps, lands far from the equator appear larger than they are.

Because they show true directions, Mercator maps are especially useful to navigators. For instance, the city of Lisbon, Portugal, lies almost exactly east of Baltimore, Maryland. A Mercator map shows that a ship could reach Lisbon by sailing from Baltimore straight east across the Atlantic Ocean.

The shortest route. Strangely enough, the best way to reach Lisbon from Baltimore is not by traveling straight east. There is a shorter route. In order to understand why this is so, you might like to perform the following experiment.

On your classroom globe, locate Lisbon and Baltimore. Both cities lie just south of the 40th parallel. Take a piece of string and connect the two cities. Let the string follow the true east-west direction of the 40th parallel. Now, draw the string tight. Notice that it passes far to the north of the 40th parallel. The path of the tightened string is the shortest route between Baltimore and Lisbon. The shortest route between any two points on the earth is called the great* circle route.

The gnomonic (nō mon′ ik) projection. Using a globe and a piece of string is not a very handy or accurate way of finding great circle routes. Instead, sailors and fliers use a special kind of map called the gnomonic projection. (See illustration H, above.) On this kind of map, the great circle route between any two places can be found simply by drawing a straight line between them.

Equal-area projections. Mercator and gnomonic maps are both very useful, but they do not show true areas. They cannot be used when you want to compare areas in different parts of the world. This is because sections of these maps that are the same size do not always represent the same amounts of the earth's surface.

Maps that do show true areas are called equal-area projections. If one square * inch of such a map represents a certain number of square miles on the earth's surface, then every other square inch of the map will represent an equal number of square miles on the earth. In order to draw an equal-area map of the world on a flat surface, the shapes of the landmasses and bodies of water must be distorted. (See illustration I, above.) To avoid this, some equal-area maps are broken, or interrupted. The breaks are arranged to fall at places that are not important. (See illustration J, above.)

SPECIAL-PURPOSE MAPS

Maps that show part of the earth. For some purposes, we prefer maps that do not show the entire surface of the earth. A map of a very small area can be drawn more accurately than a map of a large area. It can also include more details.

Illustration K, below, shows a photograph and a map of the same small part of the earth. The drawings on the map that show the shape and location of things on the earth are called symbols. The small drawing that shows directions is called a compass rose. Examples of different types of compass roses are shown in the Glossary.

Maps for special purposes. Maps can show the location of many different kinds of things. For instance, a map can show what minerals are found in certain places, or what crops are grown. A small chart that lists the symbols and their meanings is usually included on a map. This is called the legend, or key. (See map M, below.)

Symbols on some geography maps stand for the amounts of things in different places. For instance, map L, at right, gives information about the number of people in the southwestern part of the United States. The key tells the meaning of the symbols, which in this case are dots and circles.

On different maps, the same symbol may stand for different things and amounts. For example, each dot on map L stands for 10,000 persons. On other maps, a dot might represent 5,000 sheep or 1,000 bushels of wheat.

There are other ways of giving information about quantity. For example, various designs or patterns may be used on a rainfall map to indicate the areas that receive different amounts of rain each year.

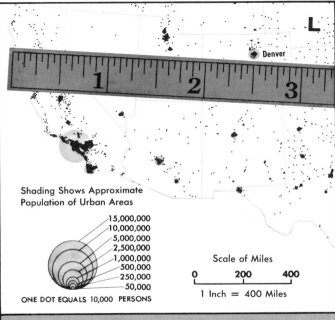

L

Denver

Shading Shows Approximate
Population of Urban Areas

15,000,000
10,000,000
5,000,000
2,500,000
1,000,000
500,000
250,000
50,000

ONE DOT EQUALS 10,000 PERSONS

Scale of Miles

0   200   400

1 Inch = 400 Miles

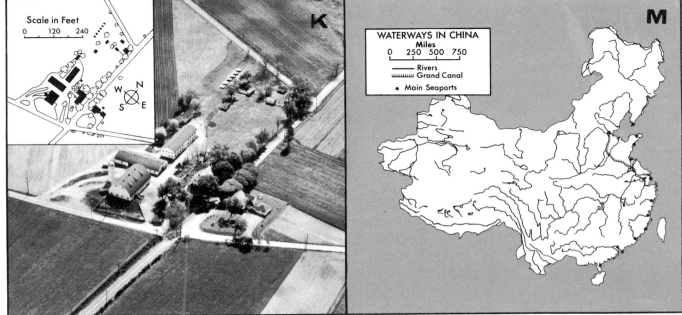

Scale in Feet

0   120   240

K

N W E S

WATERWAYS IN CHINA

Miles

0   250   500   750

— Rivers
ᴗᴗᴗᴗ Grand Canal
• Main Seaports

M

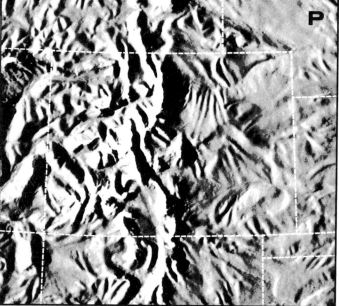

RELIEF MAPS

Some globes and maps show the roughness of the earth's surface. From a jet plane, you can see that the earth's surface is irregular. You can see mountains and valleys, hills and plains. For some purposes, globes and maps that show these things are needed. They are called relief globes and maps.

Since globes are three-dimensional models of the earth, you may wonder why most globes do not show the roughness of the earth's surface. The reason for this is that the highest mountain on the earth is not very large when it is compared with the earth's diameter. Even a very large globe would be almost perfectly smooth.

In order to make a relief globe or map, you must use a different scale for the height of the land. For example, you might start with a large flat map. One inch on your flat map represents a distance of one hundred miles on the earth. Now you are going to make a model of a mountain on your map. On the earth, this mountain is two miles high. If you let one inch represent a height of two miles on the earth, your mountain should rise one inch above the flat surface of your map. Other mountains and hills should be modeled on this same scale.

By photographing relief globes and maps, flat maps can be made that show the earth much as it looks from an airplane. Maps N and O, at the top of this page, are photographs of a relief globe. Map P is a photograph of a relief map.

Topographic maps. Another kind of map that shows the roughness of the earth's surface is called a topographic, or contour, map. On this kind of map, lines are drawn to show different heights of the earth's surface. These are called contour lines. The illustrations on this page help to explain how topographic maps are made.

Illustration Q is a drawing of a hill. Around the bottom of the hill is our first contour line. This line connects all the points at the base of the hill that are exactly twenty feet above sea level. Higher up the hill, another contour line is drawn, connecting all the points that are exactly forty feet above sea level. A line is also drawn at a height of sixty feet. Other lines are drawn every twenty feet until the top of the hill is reached. Since the hill is shaped somewhat like a cone, each contour line is shorter than the one just below it.

Illustration R shows how the contour lines in the drawing of the hill (Q) can be used to make a topographic map. This map gives us a great deal of information about the hill. Since each line is labeled with the height it represents, you can tell how high the different parts of the hill are. It is important to remember that land does not really rise in layers, as you might think when you look at a topographic map. Wherever the contour lines are far apart, you can be sure that the land slopes gently. Where they are close together, the slope is steep. With practice, you can picture the land in your mind as you look at such a map. Topographic maps are especially useful to men who design such things as roads and buildings.

On a topographic map, the spaces between the contour lines may be filled in with different shades of gray. If a different shade of gray were used for each different height of land shown in map R, there would be ten shades. It would be very hard for you to tell these different shades of gray apart. Therefore, on map S, at right, black and four shades of gray were used to show differences in height of forty feet. The key box shows the height of the land represented by the different shades. On some topographic maps, colors are used to represent different heights of land.

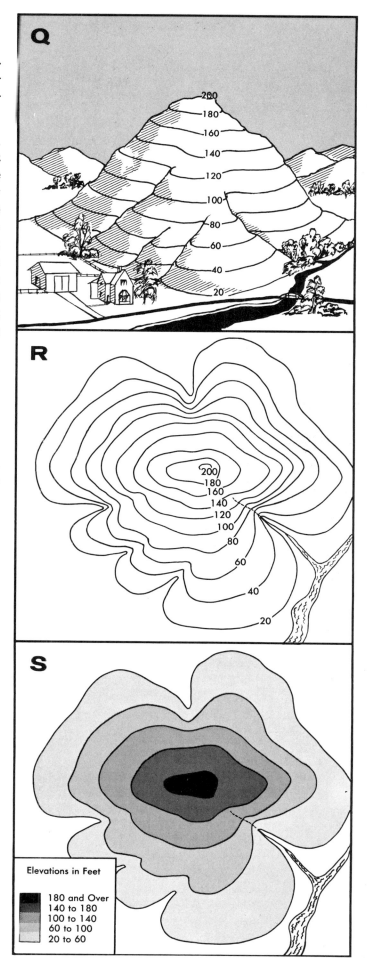

11

Learning Social Studies Skills

What is a skill? A skill is something that you have learned to do well. To learn some skills, such as swimming, you must train the muscles of your arms and legs. To learn others, such as typing, you must train your fingers. Still other skills require you to train your mind. For example, reading with understanding is a skill that requires much mental training. The skills that you use in the social studies are largely mental skills.

Why are skills important? Mastering different skills will help you to have a more satisfying life. You will be healthier and enjoy your leisure time more if you develop skills needed to take part in various sports. By developing artistic skills, you will be able to express your feelings more fully. It is even more important for you to develop skills of the mind. These skills are the tools that you will use in obtaining and using the knowledge you need to live successfully in today's world.

To develop a skill, you must practice it correctly. If you ask a fine athlete or musician how he gained his skill, he will say, "Through practice." To develop skills of the mind, you must practice also. Remember, however, that a person cannot become a good ballplayer if he keeps throwing the ball incorrectly. The same thing is true of mental skills. To master them, you must practice them correctly.

The following pages contain suggestions about how to perform correctly several important skills needed in the social studies. Study these skills carefully, and use them.

How To Find Information You Need

Each day of your life you seek information. Sometimes you want to know certain facts just because you are curious. Most of the time, however, you want information for some special purpose. If your hobby is baseball, for example, you may want to know how to figure batting averages. If you collect stamps, you need to know how to identify the countries they come from. As a student in today's world, you need information for many purposes. As an adult, you will need to gain even more knowledge in order to live successfully in tomorrow's world.

You may wonder how you can possibly learn all the facts you are going to need during your lifetime. The answer is that you can't. Therefore, knowing how to find information when you need it is of vital importance to you. Following are suggestions for locating good sources of information and for using these sources to find the facts that you need.

Written Sources of Information

1. Books. You may be able to find the information you need in books that you have at home or in your classroom. To see if a textbook or other nonfiction book has the information you need, look at the table of contents and the index.

Sometimes, you will need to go to your school or community library to locate books that contain the information you want. To make the best use of a library, you should learn to use the card catalog. This is a file that contains information about the books in the library. Each nonfiction book has at least three cards, filed in alphabetical order. One is for the title, one is for the author, and one is for the subject of the book. Each card gives the book's special number. This number will help you to find the book, since all the nonfiction books in the library are arranged on the shelves in numerical order. If you cannot find a book you want, the librarian will be glad to help you.

2. Reference volumes. You will find much useful information in special books known as reference volumes. These include dictionaries, encyclopedias, atlases, and other

special books. Some companies publish a book each year with statistics and general information about the events of the preceding year. Such books are usually called yearbooks, annuals, or almanacs.

3. Newspapers and magazines. These are important sources of up-to-date information. Sometimes you will want to look for information in papers or magazines that you do not have at home. You can usually find the ones you want at the library.

The *Readers' Guide to Periodical Literature,* which is available in most libraries, will direct you to magazine articles about the subject you are investigating. This is a series of volumes that list articles by title, author, and subject. In the front of each volume is an explanation of the abbreviations used to indicate the different magazines and their dates.

4. Booklets, pamphlets, and bulletins. Many materials of this type are available from local and state governments, as well as from our federal government. Chambers of commerce, travel bureaus, trade organizations, private companies, and embassies of foreign countries publish materials that contain a wealth of information.

Many booklets and bulletins give accurate information. You should remember, however, that some of them are intended to promote certain products or ideas. Information obtained from such sources should be checked carefully.

Reading for Information

The following suggestions will help you to save time and effort when you are looking for information in books and other written materials.

1. Use the table of contents and the index. The table of contents appears at the beginning of the book and generally is a list of the chapters in the book. By looking at this list, you can usually tell whether the book has the type of information you need.

The index is a more detailed list of the topics that are discussed in the book. It will help you locate the pages on which specific facts are discussed. In most books, the index is at the back. Encyclopedias often include the index in a separate volume, however.

At the beginning of an index, you will usually find an explanation that makes it easier to use. For example, the explanation at the beginning of the Index for *Southeast Asia* tells you that *p* means picture, and *m* means map.

The topics, or entries, in the index are arranged in alphabetical order. To locate all the information you need, you may have to look under more than one entry. For example, to find out which pages in this book contain information about cities, you might first look up the entry for cities. Then you could look up entries for individual cities in which you are interested.

2. Skim the written material to see if it contains the information you need. Before you begin reading a chapter or a page, skim it to see if it has the information you need. In this way you will not run the risk of wasting time reading something that is of little or no value to you. When you skim, you look mainly for topic headings, topic sentences, and key words. For example, imagine you are looking for the answer to the question: "How do typhoons affect farming in the Philippines?" In the Climate chapter of Part 1 of *Southeast Asia,* you might look for a topic heading that mentions the Philippines. When you find this topic heading, you might then look for the key word, "typhoon."

3. Read carefully when you think you have located the information you need. When you think you have found the page that contains the information you are looking for, read it carefully. Does it really tell you what you want to know? If not, you will need to look further.

Other Ways of Obtaining Information

1. Direct experience. What you observe or experience for yourself may be a good source of information if you have observed carefully and remembered accurately. First-hand information can often be obtained by visiting places in your community or nearby, such as museums, factories, or government offices.

2. Radio and television. Use the listings in your local newspaper to find programs about the subjects in which you are interested.

3. Movies, filmstrips, recordings, and slides. Materials on a great variety of subjects are available. They can be obtained from schools, libraries, museums, and private companies.

4. Resource people. Sometimes, you will be able to obtain information by interviewing a person who has special knowledge. On occasion, you may wish to invite someone to speak to your class and answer questions.

Evaluating Information

During your lifetime, you will constantly need to evaluate what you see, hear, and read. Information is not true or significant simply because it is presented on television or is written in a book, magazine, or newspaper. The following suggestions will help you in evaluating information.

Learn to tell the difference between primary and secondary sources of information. A primary source of information is a first-hand record. For example, a photograph taken of an event while it is happening is a primary source. So is the report you write about a field trip you take. Original documents, such as the Constitution of the United States, are primary sources also.

A secondary source is a secondhand report. For example, if you write a report about what someone else told you he saw, your report will be a secondary source of information. Another example of a secondary source is a history book.

Advanced scholars like to use primary sources whenever possible. However, these sources are often difficult to obtain. Most students in elementary and high school use secondary sources. You should always be aware that you are using secondhand information when you use a secondary source.

Find out who said it and when it was said. The next step in evaluating information is to ask, "Who said it?" Was he a scholar with special training in the subject about which he wrote? Was he a newsman with a reputation for careful reporting of the facts?

Another question you should ask is "When was it said?" Changes take place rapidly in our world, and the information you are using may be out of date. For example, many nations in Africa have won independence in recent years, so a political map of this continent that is ten years old is no longer accurate.

Find out if it is mainly fact or opinion. The next step in evaluating information is to decide whether it is based on facts or whether it mainly consists of unsupported opinions. You can do this best if you are aware of these three types of statements.

1. Statements of fact that can be checked. For example, "Voters in the United States choose their representatives by secret ballot" is a statement of fact that can be checked by observing how voting is carried on in different parts of our country.

2. Inferences, or conclusions that are based on facts. The statement, "The people of the United States live in a democracy," is an inference. This inference is based on the fact that the citizens choose their representatives by secret ballot, and on other facts that can be proved. It is important to remember that inferences can be false or only partly true.

3. Value judgments, or opinions. The statement, "It is always wrong for a country

Seven Propaganda Tricks

People who use propaganda have learned many ways of presenting information to influence you in the direction they wish. Seven propaganda tricks to watch for are listed below.

Name-calling. Giving a label that is disliked or feared, such as "un-American," to an organization, a person, or an idea. This trick often persuades people to reject something they know nothing about.

Glittering Generalities. Trying to win support by using fine-sounding phrases, such as "the best deal in town," or "the American way." These phrases have no clear meaning when you stop and think about them.

Transfer. Connecting a person, product, or idea with something that people already feel strongly about. For example, displaying a picture of a church next to a speaker to give the impression that he is honest and trustworthy.

Testimonial. Getting well-known persons or organizations to announce in public their support of a person, product, or idea.

Plain Folks. Trying to win support by giving the impression of being just an ordinary person who can be trusted. For example, a political candidate may try to win people's confidence by giving the impression that he is a good father who loves children and dogs.

Card Stacking. Giving the wrong impression by giving only part of the facts about a person, product, or idea. For example, giving favorable facts, and leaving out unfavorable ones.

Bandwagon. Trying to win support by saying that "everybody knows that," or "everyone is doing this."

---

to go to war," is a value judgment. Since a value judgment is an opinion, you need to examine it very critically. On what facts and inferences is it based? For example, what facts and conclusions do you think form the basis of the opinion, "It is always wrong for a country to go to war"? Do you agree or disagree with these conclusions? A reliable writer or reporter is careful to let his reader know which statements in his writing are his own opinions. He also tries to base his opinions as much as possible on facts that can be proved.

Find out why it was said. The next step in evaluating information is to find out the purpose for which it was prepared. Many books and articles are prepared in an honest effort to give you accurate information. For example, a scientist writing about a new scientific discovery will usually try to report his findings as accurately as possible, and he will be careful to distinguish between what he has actually observed and the conclusions he has drawn from these facts.

Some information, however, is prepared mainly to persuade people to believe or act a certain way. Information of this kind is called propaganda.

Some propaganda is used to promote causes that are generally considered good. A picture that shows Smokey the Bear and the words "Only *you* can prevent forest fires" is an example of this kind of propaganda.

Propaganda is also used to make people support causes they would not agree with if they knew more about them. This kind of propaganda may consist of information that is true, partly true, or false. Even when it is true, however, the information may be presented in such a way as to mislead you.

Propaganda generally appeals to people's emotions rather than to their reasoning ability. For this reason, you should learn to identify information that is propaganda. Then you can think about it calmly and clearly, and evaluate it intelligently.

Making Reports

There are many occasions when you need to share information or ideas with others. Sometimes you will need to do this in writing. Other times you will need to do it orally. One of the best ways to develop your writing and speaking skills is by making oral and written reports. The success of your report will depend on how well you have organized your material. It will also depend on your skill in presenting it. Here are some guidelines that will help you in preparing a good report.

Decide upon a goal. Have your purpose clearly in mind. Are you mainly interested in communicating information? Do you want to give your own viewpoint on a subject, or are you trying to persuade other people to agree with you?

Find the information you need. Be sure to use more than one source. If you are not sure how to locate information about your topic, read the suggestions on pages 12-14.

Take good notes. To remember what you have read, you must take notes. Before you begin taking notes, however, you will need to make a list of the questions you want your report to answer. As you do research, write down the facts that answer these questions. You may find some interesting and important facts that do not answer any of your questions. If you feel that they might be useful in your report, write them down, too. Your notes should be brief and in your own words except when you want to use exact quotations. When you use a quotation, be sure to put quotation marks around it.

You will be able to make the best use of your notes if you write them on file cards. Use a separate card for each statement or group of statements that answers one of your questions. To remember where your information came from, write on each card the title, author, and date of the source. When you have finished taking notes, group the cards according to the questions they answer. This will help you arrange your material in logical order.

Make an outline. After you have reviewed your notes, make an outline. This is a general plan that shows the order and the relationship of the ideas you want to include in your report. The first step in making an outline is to pick out the main ideas. These will be the main headings in your outline. (See sample outline below.) Next, list under each of these headings the ideas and facts that support or explain it. These related ideas are called subheadings. As you arrange your information, ask yourself the following questions.

a. Is there one main idea I must put first because everything else depends on it?

b. Have I arranged my facts in such a way as to show relationships among them?

c. Are there some ideas that will be clearer if they are discussed after other ideas have been explained?

d. Have I included enough facts so that I can complete my outline with a summary statement or a logical conclusion?

When you have completed your first outline, you may find that some parts of it are skimpy. If so, you may wish to do more research. When you are satisfied that you have enough information, make your final outline. Remember that this outline will serve as the basis of your finished report.

Example of an outline. The author of this feature prepared the following outline before writing "Making Reports."

I. Introduction
II. Deciding upon a goal
III. Finding information
IV. Taking notes
  A. List main ideas to be researched
  B. Write on file cards facts that support or explain these ideas
  C. Group cards according to main ideas
V. Making an outline
  A. Purpose of an outline
  B. Guidelines for arranging information
  C. Sample outline of this section
VI. Preparing a written report
VII. Presenting an oral report

Special guidelines for a written report. Using your outline as a guide, write your report. The following suggestions will help you to make your report interesting and clear.

Create word pictures that your readers can see in their minds. Before you begin to write, imagine that you are going to make a movie of the subject you plan to write about. What scenes would you like to show on the screen? Next, think of the words that will create these same pictures in your readers' minds.

Group your sentences into good paragraphs. It is usually best to begin a paragraph with a topic sentence that says to the reader, "This is what you will learn about in this paragraph." The other sentences in the paragraph should help to support or explain the topic sentence.

A sample paragraph. Below is a sample paragraph. The topic sentence has been underlined. Notice how clear it is and how well the other sentences support it. Also notice how many pictures the paragraph puts in your mind.

> Later in the day we visit a fishing village and learn how the fish are processed to keep them from spoiling. This must be done quickly, for there are no refrigerators. In one place we stop to watch some villagers mixing salt and small fish in wooden vats. The mixture will ferment and make a tasty, strong-smelling sauce that is eaten with rice and vegetables.

Other guidelines. There are two other things to remember in writing a good report. First, use the dictionary to find the spelling of words you are doubtful about. Second, make a list of the sources of information you used, and include it at the beginning or end of your report. This list is called a bibliography.

Special guidelines for an oral report. When you are going to give a report orally, you will also want to organize your information in a logical order by making an outline.

Prepare notes to guide you during your talk. These notes should be complete enough to help you remember all the points you want to make. You may even write out certain portions of your report that you prefer to read.

When you present your report, speak directly to your audience. Pronounce your words correctly and distinctly. Remember to speak slowly enough for your listeners to follow what you are saying, and use a tone of voice that will hold their interest. Stand up straight, but try not to be too stiff. Remember, the only way to improve your speaking skills is to practice them correctly.

Holding a Group Discussion

One of the important ways in which you learn is by exchanging ideas with other people. You do this frequently in informal conversation. You are likely to learn more, however, when you take part in the special kind of group conversation that we call a discussion. A discussion is more orderly than a conversation, and it usually has a definite, serious purpose. This purpose may be the sharing of information or the solving of a problem. In order to reach its goal, the discussion group must arrive at a conclusion or make a decision of some kind.

A discussion is more likely to be successful when those who take part in it observe the following guidelines.

1. Be prepared. Think about the topic to be discussed ahead of time. Prepare for the discussion by reading and taking notes. You may also want to make an outline of the ideas you want to share with the group.

2. Take part. Contribute to the discussion; express your ideas clearly and concisely. Be sure that the statements you make and the questions you ask deal with the topic being discussed.

3. Listen and think. Listen thoughtfully to others. Encourage all of the members of the discussion group to express their ideas. Do not make up your mind about a question or a problem until all of the facts have been given.

4. Be courteous. When you speak, address the entire group. Ask and answer questions politely. When you disagree with someone, point out your reasons calmly and in a friendly way.

Working With Others

In school and throughout life, you will find that there are many projects that can be done better by a group than by one person working alone. Some of these projects would take too long to finish if they were done by a single individual. Others have different parts that can be done best by people with different talents.

Before your group begins a project, you should decide several matters. First, determine exactly what you are trying to accomplish. Second, decide what part of the project each person should do. Third, schedule when the project is to be completed.

The group will do a better job and reach its goals more quickly if each person follows these suggestions.

1. Do your part. Remember that the success of your project depends on every member of the group. Be willing to do your share of the work and to accept your share of the responsibility.

2. Follow the rules. Help the group decide on sensible rules, and then follow them. When a difference of opinion cannot be settled by discussion, make a decision by majority vote.

3. Share your ideas. Be willing to share your ideas and talents with the group. When you submit an idea for discussion, be prepared to see it criticized or even rejected. At the same time, have the courage to stick up for a principle or a belief that is really important to you.

4. Respect others. Remember that every person is an individual with different beliefs and talents. Give the other members of the group a chance to be heard, and be ready to appreciate their work and ideas.

5. Be friendly, thoughtful, helpful, and cheerful. Try to express your opinions seriously and sincerely without hurting others or losing their respect. Listen politely to the ideas of others.

6. Learn from your mistakes. Look for ways in which you can be a better group member the next time you work with others on a project.

Building Your Vocabulary

When you do research in many different types of reading materials, you are likely to find several words you have never seen before. If you skip over these words, you may not fully understand what you are reading. The following suggestions will help you to discover the meanings of new words and build your vocabulary.

1. See how the word is used in the sentence. When you come to a new word, don't stop reading. Read on beyond the new word to see if you can discover any clues to what its meaning might be. Trying to figure out the meaning of a word from the way it is used may not give you the exact definition. However, it will give you a general idea of what the word means.

2. Sound out the word. Break the word up into syllables, and try to pronounce it. When you say the word aloud, you may find that you know it after all but have simply never seen it in print.

3. Look in the dictionary. When you think you have figured out what a word means and how it is pronounced, check with the dictionary. Have you pronounced it correctly? Did you decide upon the right definition? Remember, most words have several meanings. Do you know which meaning should be used?

4. Make a list of the new words you learn. In your own words, write a definition of each word you include in your list. Review this list from time to time.